Praise for Simple Faith

"*Simple Faith* is a must-read for both the new Christian and seasoned Christian alike.

A pleasurable read chock-full of timely scripture and bible doctrine. Jean Archambault-White writes about a believer's walk to Christian maturity and discovery built on Christ's unfailing love and on a basic foundation of faith—*Simple Faith.*"

—**Alison Timler, RN, LMT,** *Bayside Community Church, Bradenton, Florida*

"I cherish this awesome book. It exudes the amazing, tender love of God for His creation, how we should respond to it, and how we should surrender all to allow Him to transform our lives. No one who reads this book will ever be uncertain of the character of the God we worship, and of the urgent need to abide in Him daily. To the new Christian, it is an invaluable training ground; to those further along the journey, it is a joyous, refreshing, and oft needed reminder of the pure, good, holy things of God. It gently but firmly recalls the standard: to love God and seek Him in first place with our whole hearts; to love what God loves most, people; and to let Him take care of *all* the rest, just as He has promised."

—*Kevin Hayes, MBA, entrepreneur; lay minister, Crossroads Church, Sarasota, Florida*

"After reading *Simple Faith*, it made me hunger to spend more time with God, in His word building my faith. I was reminded of the importance of cultivating my faith by exercising and strengthening it each day. *Simple Faith* helped me to realize that we can demonstrate our faith everywhere and in everything. It truly can be that simple."

—*Valerie Ellery, teacher and Bayside Women's Ministries leader, Bayside Community Church, Bradenton, Florida*

"*Simple Faith* is phenomenal! It is such a great description of faith, the basis of our beliefs and how we should live each day of our lives. *Simple Faith* is a great witness tool to use when sharing the gospel with others. It will help someone to understand how simple our salvation and love from God is to accept and claim. Each Christian needs to have this in their library. I couldn't stop reading it!"

—*Rob Holeman, Pediatric Cardiology Clinical Research Coordinator, Duke University Hospital, and North Raleigh United Methodist Church children's church worker, Raleigh, North Carolina*

"Scripture says, 'faith is the substance of things hoped for and the evidence of things not yet seen.' Jean's life has been a faithful example of *Simple Faith* to me as she has exercised her own faith and taught me that God gives each of us our own measure of faith. God says to us, 'Trust Me, try Me, prove Me.' Even though I now have terminal cancer,

I have a peace that passes all understanding because of this faith—this easily learned *Simple Faith*."

　　—*Elizabeth T. Hall*, author, *"Caring for a Loved*
　　One with Alzheimer's: A Christian Perspective,"
　　St. Luke's Methodist Church, Memphis, Tennessee

"Don't let the title *Simple Faith* fool you. This book deals with very challenging issues of faith in a very well thought-out manner. Christians who are serious about their relationships with God would do well to consider Jean's comments ... This book should be considered by every serious student of faith."

　　—*Alex E. Anderson*, Associate Pastor, Bayside
　　Community Church, Bradenton, Florida

simple
FAITH

Tate Publishing
& Enterprises

Simple Faith

Cover design by Jen Redden
Interior design by Melissa M. Griggs
ISBN: 1–5988677–2-5
07.02.19

simple
FAITH

Jean A. Archambault-White

TATE PUBLISHING & Enterprises

Acknowledgements

My husband George for his constant love and support; Beth Hall, my "Sissie" for being my help, listening ear, prayer partner and strength; my dear friends and pastors Dave and Sue Bowman, Randy and Amy Bezet, and Jim and LaRae Crawmer for helping me walk and grow in faith; my family and George's for their prayer support and encouragement; most especially my brother Bob and sister-in-law Lisa and my sister Cathy for their special love, hospitality, and encouragement; Alison Timler for her precious love and friendship, unflagging encouragement, and generous time and help with my work; my friend DBF for her support and encouragement; Shirley and Clark Lind, my Bayside "parents"; my Bayside "sisters" Valerie Ellery and Toni Browning for their encouragement and prayers (and especially Toni for teaching me the all-important word "funnel"); Kevin Hayes for coming to NC and bringing us to Florida, for his love and friendship and his own special brand of inspiration; for all of my readers that gave generously of their time; and especially the Bayside Tuesday night intercessory prayer team for their prayers and high-fives; but more than anyone else, my LORD and Savior Jesus Christ, Who gives to me and allows me to use this talent for His glory: all glory and honor and praise be to His Name.

In loving memory of
Faith Elizabeth Taber.
A young lady of faith
December 5, 1991–April 14, 2005

Table of Contents

Simple Faith

"I saw the L<small>ORD</small> always in my presence; for He is at my right hand, so that I will not be shaken."

—*Acts 2:25*

Faith is being sure of what we hope for, a deep and abiding, unshakeable conviction, a knowing. Faith says, "I *know*" when others say, "I hope so." Faith is the thing in your spirit planted there by the Holy Spirit of God that is so deeply embedded that it can't be uprooted. Faith says believing in God is imperative, essential, and not an option. Faith is that part of you that tells you that what others think might be true is a fact, plain and simple.

Faith is an amazing thing. Just as some people may say that an illness is "all in your head," faith is "all in your spirit." When I wake up in the morning I think about the day ahead and all I have to do, and these thoughts gradually turn into prayers of faith. I think through what I must do, where I must go, and whether or not I'll be able to accomplish these things this day, and my thoughts and prayers then become actions. And so it is, with whatever energy God gives me for today, I take up the day's journey secure in one basic truth: faith can be a simple matter. I need only lean on God, trust Him, believe what He says and He will lead me wherever this day takes me, in wherever I need to go, in whatever I need to do. This is simple—this faith. God only asks that we take Him at His word, that we only believe that He loves us and wants His best for us.

God has a wonderful plan for your life and you don't have to spend your whole life trying to figure out what it is, you don't have to labor all your life trying to discover what it is. It's not some big cosmic deal. You need to simply love Him, to seek Him in His Word and prayer, to do your best to obey Him. God, in return, will give you joy and blessing beyond what you would ever dream possible. He will walk with you every day of your life, meeting you at every turn in the road. He will lift you up, carry you through your troubles, give you peace and prosperity, and show Himself always faithful. He will be your God if you will turn yourself over to Him. He loves you beyond anything you can imagine, and He wants you to exercise faith in Him. He wants to answer your prayers, and He wants you to know Him in an intimate way. He wants you to come to Him; He wants to be your Father and He wants you to be His child, to know Him as you would know your own beloved parents. He wants to hold you in His arms when you are weary and troubled. He wants to delight you with His love. In return, He asks that you live a life tuned in to Him, that you trust Him and love Him, that you praise Him and worship Him, that you give back to Him a portion of what He gives you. That's not much to ask for what He gives you, is it?

God understands our human hearts intimately, that we are not perfect in and of ourselves. That's not what He asks or expects of us. He only asks that we do our best, that we only try and then ask forgiveness when we fall short. We don't have to struggle and strive in order to be good enough to earn all of this that God offers. He takes us just as we are. Faith is enough. Simple faith is the key, even if it's just little, tiny faith. Faith is what we need to succeed in every facet of our lives. God has made each of us as a unique and special individual with a distinct purpose, each designed specifically for what He has in mind for our lives alone. He has then equipped each of us with the exact measure of faith needed to fulfill that unique purpose for which He has created us.

" … as God has allotted to each a measure of faith for, just as we have many members in one body and all the members do not have the same function, so we, who are many, are one body in Christ, and individually members one of another" (Romans 12:3–5).

My faith enables me to keep walking with God, seeking Him, growing in Him, becoming more like Him every day. Eventually, even if it's after this life is all over, I'll be exactly as God created me to be, all I need to be according to His unique plan for my life alone. Even if I can't impact all the people I'm meant to while I'm here, my best efforts blessed by God may mean that my words will finally sink in after I'm gone. That's what we strive for—that's why we should always try to do our best.

The whole point of faith is that we don't need the things of the world to get by. We don't need the measuring sticks of the world to decide whether we're making it, whether we're "good enough," whether we have what it takes. King David, known for having "a heart after the LORD," kept his eyes always upward, always on the LORD and His plan for his life. Oh David stumbled, sometimes phenomenally, but he always got up when he fell down, then fell once again, next to his knees, pleading with God to renew him. God always honored those prayers, forgave David's sins and redeemed him again—and again and again. The book of Psalms records David's constant struggles with his sins and failings, and his tortured prayers as he returned repentantly to God.

They record also his exultations, his joy and his ecstasy as God forgave him, assisted him and loved him faithfully and continually, never turning His back on David. God does the same for each of us when we come back to Him time and again, as long as our hearts are truly contrite and regretful of our sin, and we truly love the LORD—as long as our prayers are sincere. We must try time and again to obey God, to do better, to grow in Him, to avoid sin with all that is in us. That's what faith is all about.

Simply put, faith says, "I know my God is a living God—I know He lives and that He is there for me all the time—no matter what."

Of course we don't purposely set out to sin, we don't willfully turn from God and do wrong—such is not faith. But we *are* born sinners; we sin continually despite our best efforts. But those of us who try to maintain the attitude of the pure in heart say, "Your promises have been thoroughly tested and your servant loves them" (Psalm 119:140).

This is how we operate in faith, how we manage our earthly lives day by day. We follow God through His Word, we pursue Him in prayer and worship; we try and fail, we turn back to Him time and again. So I say again, this faith can be a simple matter. You believe. Period. You believe because God says to believe. You believe because you are told by God, by Jesus Himself, to believe. You believe because you are taught by God's Word to believe. You believe because you see things (little miracles, in fact) that help you believe, you hear things (testimonies) that reinforce your belief. By and by your faith grows, because God helps you believe. You walk with God and something in you responds to God, to the things He promises, because He makes them happen even if it's in the smallest of things. This is the Holy Spirit within you guiding you back to God, keeping you right there with God where you belong.

Faith is simple—it's cause and effect. You pray, and your prayers are answered. Faith is simple, like planting seeds and watching flowers and vegetables come up. If you apply water (more prayer) and fertilizer (the prayers of others) some sunshine (prayers answered, some positive declarations about what God has done and is now doing in your life), the crop flourishes—even sometimes grows wild like wildflowers. Faith is simple like the growth of a child. Nurture it and it grows big and strong. Like a muscle, if it is exercised diligently and often, it becomes toned and strong.

Unused, faith becomes weak and flabby, drooping, lifeless, and useless—it withers. Like a muscle, faith can occasionally accomplish great feats when bathed with a sort of spiritual desperation akin to physical adrenaline—like a mother lifting the front end of a car off her child to save his life. Such circumstances may be rare, for such strong faith is rare—though it need not be. True, strong faith comes through faithful living and "faith comes by hearing and hearing by the Word of God . . ." (Romans 10:17). Staying close to God strengthens one's faith. He is found through His Word; His presence is found in worship and prayer. We must seek it every day.

A friend who says she is "a believer" is not sure she believes in eternity. I am not sure what she believes at all. In the church? Or in Christ? This I must be diligent to investigate; her soul may be in danger. But how can I answer her, help her? When I see her, our time is so limited—it's almost as if our meetings are in passing—just a few words and then we must part. How can I make her understand that Jesus is doing what He said, making a place for us in eternity?

Jesus told His disciples, "In My Father's house are many

rooms; if it were not so, I would have told you. I am going there to prepare a place for you. And if I go and prepare a place for you, I will come back and take you to be with Me there, that you also may be where I am" (John 14:2–3).

First I need to make sure she understands that faith or belief in a church isn't what God wants from us. It's *relation-ship* with Him, with Christ, that is what He wants. What can I say to introduce this topic of faith, to get to the root of her basic view or philosophy of faith? How can she believe in eternity if she doesn't even know to believe in the One Who is preparing for her stay there? I pray for a time when an opening comes, when we can talk a while.

We must not show ourselves afraid in our faith but instead show ourselves strong, show ourselves "approved" (II Timothy 2:15). We must study and know the Word of God, but most of all, we must demonstrate our faith. We must know what we believe, then show it and be ready to help others believe. We must equip ourselves with a loving compassion that is bold, that stops people in their tracks, that pulls them up short, that confronts them with their need for Christ. Every soul *must* have Christ; there is no other way to God.

Each of us, even "good" people, must understand our sinful natures—must see and understand what we battle in the flesh, in our humanness. Has any one of us stolen anything? Yes. Lied? Yes. Blasphemed? Yes. Hated? The Word of God says to harbor hatred in the heart toward someone is the same as murder (Matthew 5:22). To look at someone with lust in the heart is the same as committing adultery (Matthew 5:28). So each of us is guilty. Just as we go to court and stand before a judge and hear "guilty" pronounced and have sentence passed upon us, so must each of us stand one day before God. He will judge us for our sins by His holy standard and say the same: "guilty." The punishment is death. God will turn His holy face away from this guilt, this sin, this unholiness. He will tell us to depart from Him; He cannot bear unholiness. The sinful cannot enter the perfect holiness of God's presence.

So then the sinful are condemned and are to take their place in the lake of fire. Unless … Our Father cannot bear to see His children lost for eternity. We were made to praise Him, to fellowship with Him. We were made to spend eternity with Him. So He pays our bail. He pays the whole fine. He has made a way. The eternal Judge pays the fine, at an enormous cost, the price of life for life, His Son for all of these who will otherwise be lost. How can we be worthy, for we are, indeed not?

No, we cannot be worthy. So we accept this magnificent gift, this ransom of One for many, for all the sinners of all time. We come by an invitation open to all who will accept the gift freely given and have only to say, "Yes! I accept!"

It is the only way for us, we who are liars, blasphemers, thieves, adulterers, murderers. We are all guilty; none of us are able to enter God's presence, for we have all broken faith with God, broken His commands. We are all unholy. So we must accept this magnificent gift by simple faith alone, for we have nothing to give in return. We are then spared, we are saved. (See *How to Become a Christian*.)

Instead of God saying, "I never knew you," Christ welcomes us and says, "This one is mine." A simple plan, perfect in its simplicity; one sacrifice for all mankind, one sacrifice for all time. (See the chapter *Access to God through Faith*.)

Faith and our walk with the LORD is like any other thing in our lives. If you care about something, if it's worthwhile to you, you pay attention to it. Do you know more about, say, your favorite baseball team or golfer, your job, politics, or TV shows than about what the Bible has to say on a critical issue? Do you know what the Bible says about today's issues? About feminism, the New Age movement, "modern" sexuality, politics, your finances? Are you more zealous to perform to your utmost on the job, to be the best student, the best team player, the best parent you can be, to be an exemplary citizen, yet base your beliefs and your faith on clichés and hearsay?

One woman I know has steadfastly refused to have a Christmas tree saying the Bible taught against it. When I questioned her closely about it, she couldn't remember where she had read it. After a half hour's discussion, we finally traced it back to Scriptures about sin in the Old Testament because of "high places and Asherah poles" which were altars and places of worship to false, foreign gods (one example: I Kings 14:23). Even though she saw the error, she still can never enjoy a Christmas tree and brought up her children, now all middle age, to be resistant not only to Christmas festivities but to holiday trimmings of any sort—a hardship on their families who like to decorate and celebrate.

This is only one example of misunderstanding. Another example of ignorance of God's Word is, "cleanliness is next to godliness." This also is not in the Bible. Then there's, "money is the root of all evil." The true quote is, "The *love* of money is the root of all evil" (I Timothy 6:10). Money is a thing that can be mighty useful to the work of the LORD, and can do a lot of good. Let's not condemn that.

Clichés and misquotes are sometimes downright foolish. God's pure Word is so far from that, so much more precious. Know what you're basing your faith on, and make sure it's the truth. Then you'll have a strong basis and your faith, like a plant set out in good soil, will flourish and grow healthy and strong, bearing much "fruit in season"—making your prayers and study count for much, not just here on earth but throughout eternity because of those you will help to bring along into eternity through your diligence.

Get your facts straight so you won't be afraid to answer, so you won't be caught without the knowledge of the LORD you proclaim to know and love so much. Learn to be quiet in the LORD and understand His ways and He will always lead you and provide His wisdom through your faith. Read and study the Word of God on a daily basis and join a body of believers where you'll be taught and led properly. (See the chapter *Faith to be Led.*)

I hear too many people say, "I've read the Bible plenty. I remember what it says. I don't need to read it anymore."

I've been reading my Bible for 29 years this year and every day I learn something new. That's the thing about the deep, abiding wisdom of God. You'll never fully explore the entire depths of God's holy Word, you'll never learn it all. There's always something fresh. Do you remember everything you learned in school? Of course not. We all need refreshers every day. So it is with the Word of God; there is fresh, new wisdom every day.

As for going to church, I weary of hearing people say, "I went to church every Sunday when I was growing up. I've had enough."

Did you eat three meals a day too? Had enough of that? Everyone needs a church where they can learn and grow and be groomed to work for God.

The world is changing every day and if you think you can reach people with the same evangelistic tools that you got just a few short years ago, you are sadly mistaken. Pastors should be specialists in reaching their communities, in bringing in the souls in the area entrusted to them by God. Trust your pastor(s) to lead you in reaching your own area. Trust them to counsel you, to help you, to lead you. In this way you will be fit for service and when someone challenges your faith, you'll have your answers ready or at least be able to get them quickly. If you're not getting that in your church, don't sleep through service or stay home. Find a church where you'll fit, where you feel comfortable, where you can relate to the people and understand the message being given out. (See the chapter *Faith to Be Led.*)

When your faith begins to grow, begin to exercise it. Consider the prophet Elijah in the Old Testament (I Kings 15:34–16:24). Elijah had told the people that because of their sin it would not rain until they repented. Drought followed, hard and long. He trusted God to fulfill these words of faith and God did. That is how God designed faith to work. After this and many other great feats in the LORD's name, Elijah was worn out and weary. When wicked Queen Jezebel threatened his life, this news got back to Elijah. Elijah's response at this was to flee for his life, complaining to God: "I have been very zealous for the Lord God Almighty. The Israelites have rejected Your covenant, broken down Your altars … *I am the only one left and they are trying to kill me too . . .*" (I Kings 19:10, niv).

Elijah was so exhausted that he lost all perspective and with it went his faith. Faith didn't seem so simple anymore. He was tired, he needed a rest. Just before this, Elijah had fallen asleep under a solitary tree and had awakened praying, asking God to take his life. Then he went back to sleep. He was that weary. Then God woke him and provided him a meal (I Kings 19:3–7). So Elijah ate and was refreshed and journeyed on. On the strength of this refreshment, Elijah continued through the drought another forty days and forty nights. Such is the strengthening power of God's miraculous provision, so far beyond man's!

Because Elijah found within himself enough faith to turn himself over to God again, his strength was restored. (See the chapter *Recharging Your Faith.*) Earlier, God had sent ravens to feed Elijah (I Kings 17), and then had sent him to a poor widow who was herself nearly starving. Elijah asked her for bread, and she said she had only enough for a last meal for her son and herself. But she must have sensed within Elijah the special presence of God through the power of faith and, because of it, God's ability to do something miraculous, for she obeyed. Elijah had seen God perform many miracles—setting soaking wet sacrifices on fire, slaying enemy armies, bringing the dead back to life. Despite all of these great miracles, still Elijah's faith weakened when he was exhausted. Faith can be as simple as obedience, like the widow's, like Noah's. Hebrews 11:7 says that Noah's obedience in building the ark (imagine the ridicule *he* withstood!) condemned the others around him who did not believe God.

Faith in itself is a simple precept. *Only believe.* In Jesus' day, a man came to Him seeking healing for his son who was plagued by seizures. Jesus' disciples did not want the father to bother Jesus, for they had already tried to heal the boy and perhaps thought that he could not be healed. Jesus began to talk to the boy's father and to discuss the problem with him. After some discussion, Jesus told the man that all that was needed was faith.

The man answered that he *had* faith and added, "Help my unbelief!" (Mark 9:24).

Jesus, of course, healed the boy, and rebuked the disciples for their lack of faith, then explained that they would have been able to heal the boy with the proper prayer and fasting (Mark 9:17–29). Sometimes our lack of answer to prayer is due to our focus on the many distractions of life rather than on what we may perceive as God's failure to answer us. At these times we must stop where we are and get our attention, our focus, back on God were it belongs.

My friend who wonders about eternity is laden with sadness, worry, and many cares. She has lost dear ones she hopes to see again in eternity, but she holds little hope for eternity. How can I help her if she doesn't even have hope for today? She needs immediate relief, but I don't know how to communicate to her that beginning right now, where she is with Jesus *is* immediate relief. He will take her burdens and help her carry them right now. Only Jesus can refresh her spirit, renew her soul, and reunite her with these loved ones in eternity. Her issues with eternity are common. So many will not take the time to confront their questions and seek God for the answer found only in Him. Today, many are so laden with cares that they can't see beyond them. But God has the answer they seek, and that answer is Jesus Christ whom we accept through faith. This gift from God is the answer to all our needs. It is an uncomplicated thing—to accept Jesus in faith, to accept this gift of salvation that God holds out to us. How much easier it is to bear our burdens, when they are shared with Christ!

In the Old Testament, God tried over and over to keep His people walking with Him.

Finally He said:"They are [a nation] without sense, there is no discernment in them. If only they were wise and would understand this and what their end would be!" (Deuteronomy 23:28)

How much this sounds like our own world today as it heads hell-bent and pellmell toward evident destruction. Our younger generation seems more involved today, more centered, more caring, and more interested in the world than ever before. But are they really? What is the true focus of these youth? The proverb, "There is nothing new under the sun," (Ecclesiastes 1:9) keeps repeating itself down through the ages. Our youth focus on helping the needy, feeding the hungry, saving the endangered species, saving the planet— all good things, but not the most crucial. Recently I heard that only 4% of the population between the ages of 13 and 23 profess to be Christians. They are growing up without Jesus. This terrifies me, and it should you, especially measured against the thought that it is best to reach youth for Christ before they are 12 years of age. If that doesn't speak of the desperate state of the souls of the world, then I don't know what does. What this generation needs to be focused on, what you and I need to be focused on, is saving souls, *not* "endangered species." It is mankind that is the truly endangered species.

When I think of the majority of the young people under 30 that I know (including those professing to be Christians) I think of their values and see the same errors, the same pitfalls, the same besetting sins that have plagued the world through its history. Still there is "no one holy, no, not one" (Romans 3:21–24)—no one after God's heart. All are sinful, all are astray, seeking their own interests, generation after generation as ever before. No, we are not holy—and we don't even seem to try. In fact, we go too far in the opposite direction (See *Appendix III: Paganism in Our Homes*). How can God continue to put up with us? How can this world continue spinning out of control without spinning off course and colliding with eternity?

We think that this current world with all its ungodliness and self-seeking egocentrism is something new, but it's not. It's something that has wearied God from time immemorial. Human nature has never changed. If you don't believe it, take a trip to large museum and have a look at the antiquities. You'll find plenty of little bronze and clay "household gods." It's no secret. Generation upon generation down through time has spent themselves upon their vanities—jewels, gold, costly garments, beautiful artifacts—temporal wealth recorded in paintings and lists of goods. And we're still at it.

We live in fine homes fit for kings and the earth reels out of control with our wasteful living. Children around the world are still starving, are still beaten and abused; our elders die and slide forgotten into hell unprayed-for and unwanted.

If it seems like things are getting worse, well, they probably are. Recently in the Gulf of Mexico some unknown death struck and decimated over 1,200 square miles of the water. Everything—*everything*—died and our experts don't know why. In April 2006 some devastating fungus swept worldwide even into some supposedly pristine areas leaving "piles of dead" frogs, toads and salamanders; scientists went out to capture some of the surviving creatures to try to save many species. Cape Canaveral recently released a report that says that on April 23, 2036 a 1,000 foot wide asteroid could well hit the earth with enough force to obliterate a small state. A direct hit by this force would be greater than Hurricane Katrina that destroyed New Orleans, Louisiana in 2005, the 2004 Asian tsunami and the 1906 San Francisco earthquake combined (Michael Cabbage, *Knight Ridder Tribune Service* May 15, 2006), equal to 880 million tons of TNT or 65,000 times the power of the atomic bomb dropped on Hiroshima. And, they say, the odds (1-in-6,250) are not so small, since it is calculated that asteroids this size hit the earth once every one thousand years. Added to these disasters are the seemingly escalating hurricanes, tsunamis, floods, wildfires, pestilences—and added to that are the terrorist attacks and the surrender of Israel's territories to their enemies. (See *Appendix II: World News*)

Although this sounds like doom and gloom, I am not a "doomsayer" and I am not about to tell you the world is coming to an end on such and such a date, for I have no idea and don't pretend to even guess about these things. It has ever been thus and it will never change, for the nature of man has never changed and never will until the coming of the King to deliver us finally into the eternal kingdom.

The one thing I can tell you with certainty is that we live in an evil world and that God said that when the whole world has heard His Word, the end will come. Nearly all the world now has advanced telecommunications and access to the Word in some form—printed, verbal or electronic—so I think that day is coming, and soon. That's what I believe. A date? Who knows but God? If Jesus couldn't say (" … but of that day or hour no one knows, not even the angels in heaven, nor the Son, but the Father alone . . ." (Mark 13:32)), who am I or any human being to hazard a guess? Yet why ignore things that we feel in our spirits and hearts to be true (Mark 13:27–29)? Why should we ignore what our logic and intellect tell us seem right? God has told us in His Word to be aware of certain signs that will precede the return of Christ. Among them will be certain events in the Middle East, certain things such as that all mankind will hear the Word (See *Appendix II: World News*). We can't ignore these things, and these things should make us sit up and pay attention, then leap up and into action. How can anyone who is awake and aware of today's enmity among the nations not be afraid for the state of the world and the impending end? Pick up your Bible and your newspaper and sign onto the Internet and compare what the Word of God and today's news have to say that line up with prophesy. Then compare what is being uncovered through modern archaeology that points back to Christ and the Bible and back to the early days of man.

It takes guts to live by faith, to say to someone, "I know it to be true because God says so and I stand by that. God will come through. I trust Him for that."

It takes guts to look at what seems inevitable, such as a looming house payment and a zero bank balance and say, "God will provide."

It takes guts to stick by your standards, even when someone is not looking. It takes guts to live a life of no compromise, even when it's much easier to let it go, to follow the crowd, to back down. But that's not what faith says we are to do. We stand because that's what Christ would do. We stand because that's what faith says we are to do. We stand because in faith we can—we must. Faith is what says we belong to God.

Hebrews 12:1 says we are surrounded by a great cloud of witnesses and so should throw off whatever hinders our beliefs in order to rid ourselves of the sins that weigh us down. We need this focus so that our faith can be perfected, so we may be fitted for our work. Instead of considering Jesus as God here on earth, we need to realize what He was really doing. He was here as the example of a perfect *man,* not as God. Too many people miss this.

When something is said about the way Jesus conducted Himself here, they say, "But He was God."

Yes—but no. Jesus came to earth as a human being. He laid aside His deity; He became man for the duration of His life on earth. It was only after He died and rose again that He once again took up His deity and was once more glorified and became God on earth in human form. When He walked with His apostles and disciples and taught and fellowshipped here on earth before His death, He was as human as any of us. This is critical for us to understand; it is crucial for us to have this perspective. It is essential that we know that Jesus was a man, human as we are. Otherwise His life here was pointless. For how can God know what it feels like to be a man? How can God show us how to live like a man? How could He *know?*

Jesus' success on earth was based on His faith. My own faith is how I came to write this book. A writer is always instructed to write what she knows. Before this I wrote drama; that's what I knew. I wrote for children—I know children. Now I write about faith because faith has shaped my life, made me what I am. Faith is a thing that wells up in me. It is something I cultivated with a purpose, something that was sown in me by my heavenly Father from the moment He created me. This faith is something that I recognize as a commodity to be invested, protected, used to advantage, exercised daily, shared, and freely given, as God so freely gave it to me to help me survive in this Christian walk of mine.

This faith I have is the specific amount of faith that God gives me for what I have to live through in my life alone. It is for this particular life and what it holds, not for anyone else's life. I have to use it and groom it, to care for it, feed it and water it. I could have buried it and let it rot and die, never using it. Instead, I took what God gave me and asked Him to strengthen it, and He honored that and that has helped me to use it in this, *my* life.

Faith has shaped my life. It has led me down right paths, led me away from erroneous ones, saved me from death, kept me to purpose, called me home. I can say with the apostle Paul—though never to his extent! (II Corinthians 11)—that I have suffered trials and tribulations, depression, illness, persecution, rejections, homesickness, loneliness, and many other negative things all in pursuit of the gospel. But I have never turned back from following Christ because I have had faith in Him, in His redeeming grace, in Father God and in the Holy Spirit.

My life is based on Jesus, based on what I learn from Him, based on what He made me to be. Jesus lived and walked the earth to be an example of the success that we can each be if we walk in faith. He was the perfect man of faith. He demonstrated His faith by remaining unencumbered by the world (Matthew 8:20); by separating Himself from others to recharge (Mark 1:35–36); by surrounding Himself with others whose faith was strong (Mark 5:40–42). We can be victorious through our faith by following His example.

The enemy was there tempting Jesus from the first, in the form of the devil in Jesus' temptation in the desert (Matthew 4:8–10); through the people trying to make Him king (John 6:14–16); through Peter trying to hold Him back in safety (Matthew 16:22–24); to those calling out to Him to get Himself down from the cross (Matthew 27:42; Mark 15:31; Luke 23:35). Through all of these Jesus remained steadfast to the mission He submitted Himself to and agreed to with the Father from before the foundation of the world. Psalm 110:1 shows this plan: "The LORD said to my LORD, 'Sit at My feet until I make Your enemies a footstool for Your feet.'"

How then, if Jesus, the Son of God, One with the Father and Spirit, could not operate without faith, can we ever hope to do so? As long as I walk with Jesus the Messiah in faith, as long as I claim God as my God and live accordingly, I will not be asked to carry the sin of the world on my back. I will not even, because of Jesus' forgiveness, be asked to answer for my own sin. How awesome is that forgiveness! How little He asks in return! It has all been paid for and I am redeemed. I have a free pass; my admission to heaven is paid.

This is the free gift Jesus offers, given when we say only, "I believe and I accept." (See *How to Become a Christian.*) All else follows by faith.

II Chronicles 15:2 says, "The LORD is with you when you are with Him."

That's a strong promise. So, I go looking for Him every day, and I find Him and cling to Him. Then I know I'm safe, I'm on the right path, and I can go about my business. The details will come into focus. Without all this that He went through, Jesus could not have completed His mission and we would remain lost. There would be no forgiveness for sin; there would be no acceptable sacrifice for anyone but the Jews at the altar in the holy of holies, under the strict Old Testament laws.

That is the difference between living *with* Jesus and faith because of God's grace—unmerited favor—and living *without* Jesus and faith.

With God all things are possible (Matthew 19:25–27; Mark 9:22–24; Mark 10:26–28). That's how I maintain my perspective, and that's the hope I hang on to. It's all I've got to carry me into eternity. It is *everything* that I carry into eternity. I can take nothing else with me.

Each generation produces its own outstanding men and women of faith, and I am privileged to know some of these. Ultimately, that is what saves each and every one of us Christians, keeps us going on, keeps our sanity intact when we view the awesome responsibility that we have before us, to bring the rest of the lost home to Jesus. It's faith, simple faith—faith in our heavenly Father, in the salvation that Jesus Christ secured for us by His selfless sacrifice on the cross, in the empowering life we have in the Holy Spirit.

Without it, we are lost. With it, we can do this, we can conquer what's left of the world and bring in the last of the souls that are destined to be recorded in the Lamb's Book of Life (Revelation 20:12).

This is a handbook about faith, so let us begin by turning our attention to Hebrews 11. There are listed there a few men and women of God; though the list is small, the works are memorable. As an exercise in faith-building, I strongly recommend you take the time to learn the stories that earned them mention on these pages of divine history. They lived lives of faith yet died without seeing the fulfillment of what they waited for, yet they remained steadfast.

The chapter closes with a magnificent thought: "Therefore, God is not ashamed to be called their God . . ."(Hebrews 11:16, NIV).

Oh, that God would make my life the same! When I think of that statement, I wonder what I could do to be included in such a wondrous mention. May our Father not only never be ashamed of me, but may I in some way make my life count, may I in some way make my LORD glad that He made me. May I count for something that makes Him not only unashamed, but perhaps even a little proud to call me "daughter," to be counted as one of His through whom life was lived in faith and "weakness turned to strength" (Hebrews 11:34). But I will not sit and write a retelling of the Bible, merely point you to these stories so you can read for yourself and see that when we operate in faith and trust God, He delights in freeing His power for our benefit that the "kingdom may come on earth as it is in heaven."

Jesus told His disciples, "Ask and it will be given to you, seek and you will find; knock and the door will be opened to you. For everyone who asks receives, he who seeks finds;

and to him who knocks, the door will be opened" (Luke 11:9–10).

Jesus pointed out that man, being imperfect and sinful, desires to give good things to his children and loved ones—so then, how much more would our perfect, heavenly Father desire to give us, His beloved children, good things? He especially says this concerning the Holy Spirit, Whom He promises the Father will send to help us. Through the Holy Spirit we are strengthened in our relationship with the Father, becoming more intimate with Him, and therefore living more Christ-like lives. We can know God more fully and can learn more of Him, trusting Him more each day— and this builds our faith. With the Holy Spirit guiding us, dwelling in us, faith becomes a simple matter—so easy. So let us grow in faith, let us build on this simple faith.

Seeds of Faith

*"Before I formed you in the womb I knew you ... before you were
born I set you apart ..."*

—*Jeremiah 1:5, NIV*

Long before we are born, God implants deep within each
of us tiny seeds of faith. He makes each of us unique so
each of us understands Him, knows Him in a way only we
can. Each one of us has a special, distinct, exclusive, and
personal relationship with our God and Father that no one
else has—precisely because there is no one else like each of
us. Thus when I say that I love God, that God loves me, that
He understands me and that I know Him, I can't make that
a reality for you in the same way that it is for me, no matter
how hard I try.

When I was a little girl, perhaps 7 or 8 years old, I knelt
one day in a Catholic confessional and very seriously asked
God to take away my sins. I remember that day as though it
happened yesterday and I will treasure it in my heart forever.
Few have heard me tell of it, for it is sacred to me and I do
not speak of it. When I was grown and became a Christian
in earnest and began to study the Scriptures, I read of how
Mary observed Jesus and how she treasured what she saw
of Him in her heart. I understand Mary's feeling because of
that event in my life.

On that cold winter's day, I knelt on my dark side of the confessional to confess my childish sins. I was in the church down the sidewalk from the Catholic school where I attended school from grades one through six. I don't imagine my sins were many, as I was not a particularly naughty child, and most of my sins were born more of compulsiveness rather than true wickedness.

I knelt there and received my absolution (forgiveness of sin after confession), was assigned my penance, and prayed for forgiveness. Suddenly, I saw heaven opened and a brilliant Being with flowing hair and a beard "white like wool," as the Scriptures say (Revelation 1:14). His eyes were like a golden fire. He was surrounded by swirling clouds and light—and I could really see no more than that other than that His arms rested upon the arms of a throne.

I do not think that at that time I had seen an artistic depiction of this type for I was very young, but I understood this to be God. I was awed. I went back to my place among my classmates and knelt down, and squeezing my eyes tight shut, I said my prayers diligently. I told no one what had happened.

Thus began the spiritual odyssey that was my path, my stumbling way toward my God. I continued in Catholic school where I memorized my catechisms (religious lessons) as I was expected to. When I was in the third or fourth grade I came (timid though I still was) toe to toe with a teacher who told me I "blasphemed" when I said I "understood" the Trinity of God, Who, she said, was a divine mystery.

Yes, I understood that God was One unified Person made up of Three perfect, though separate, Beings. Three in One. In my childish mind I believed that it was simple to understand God. I understand today that God's Personhood is Divine and mysterious, but I also believe I carry within me the divine revelation that He gave me at that same time of Who He is—that He gives each of us who seek Him.

God the Father and God the Son are one and the same, yet two separate Persons. Christ is the bodily representation of God, the Person we can see, the One we can relate to, for He is the perfection that God says He wants us to be—the Standard. Christ is also the Mediator, a go-between or negotiator, the Intermediary, the Moderator. Because people could actually see Christ, because He will appear again for all to see, we can identify with Him. Christ walked the earth as man and suffered all things as we do—the temptation to sin (yet did not), pain, rejection, death. He also experienced the victory we can experience—and all this through faith in God, not because He is God, for He shed His deity when He took the form of a man. Simply put, Jesus is God wearing a body. The Holy Spirit is the spirit of love that unites the two, the Father and the Son, and is ever-present with us everywhere. The Holy Spirit is the Comforter, that part of God that enables us to function in faith as God promises we can. The Holy Spirit is God Who is ever with us, ever-present.

Although God said that no one could see His face and live, He made provision for this with those He was closest to. In the Garden of Eden, He walked with Adam, appeared as "one like the Son of Man" in the Old Testament. Some of these appearances were of angels but some were clearly of God in the flesh, beginning with God walking with Adam and Eve in the Garden of Eden (Genesis 3); through Jacob's wrestling with someone (Genesis 32:25); to the LORD's appearance to John on the Island of Patmos (Revelation 1:13). One excellent example of God's appearance in the flesh in the Old Testament is in Genesis 18:1–19. God appeared to Abraham and announced that he and Sarah would have a son, that Abraham would father a mighty nation. It is clear that this is an appearance by God in the flesh by the fact that Abraham addresses Him as "Lord" and that the Lord then says to His companions, "Shall we hide from Abraham what I am about to do?" (Genesis 18:17) (God was about to utterly destroy Sodom and Gomorrah, and because Abraham's relative Lot was there, God had compassion on Abraham and told him what He was about to do.) I believe that this was God "incarnate"—in the flesh—in the same way that Jesus took on flesh in the New Testament days.

In Exodus 34:6, the Bible says, "Then the Lord passed by in front of him (Moses) and proclaimed, 'The Lord, the Lord God, compassionate and gracious, slow to anger, and abounding in lovingkindness and truth … '"

Someone appeared with Shadrach, Meshach and Abednego in the fiery furnace when they defied the king, refused to worship him and his image and proclaimed that God was able to save them. All present saw not only the three youths that were thrown into the furnace but a fourth as well, all four "walking around unbound and unharmed," one of them "like the son of gods" (Daniel 3:25).

Although the Bible tells us that no man can see God and live, there have been specific circumstances when God has made Himself compatible with what man is able to tolerate in the physical body—able to see and yet live.

There are so many instances of visitors from heaven carrying messages. Some came in dreams, some in visions, some came in bodily form. Some of these instances are hard to read; some could be angels, some could be God in the Person of Jesus before His ministerial life began. This is an important point because it is a reinforcement of the concept of the Son of God being present with God in eternity, working beside Him, always as one with Him.

The Holy Spirit of God is the same in Power as the Father and the Son, and one with them. Jesus Christ says He will send His Spirit (John 16:7–8) to help us, to guide us, to convict and direct us. The Holy Spirit is the one left to be with us after the work of the Son was completed. He is the One Who now directs us as we operate in faith, living out our lives in the New Covenant. He is the "co-pilot" that keeps us on course, the equalizer that keeps us balanced and on an even keel as we navigate life's paths.

It is the simple faith of a little child who understands how to accept at face value what God says. So it seems that being told not to question a divine mystery did in fact do some good rather than harm as I stood firm in what I knew in my childish heart. Because I was told not to question these things I instead pondered them more for I was so puzzled by being told that I was not to think on it. And what I finally understood made me surer than ever in what I knew about God: God is Who I know Him to be because He *showed* me Who He is. My idea of Who God is was fixed in my heart, soul, and spirit when I was a child, and that idea has never changed.

Before Christ left the earth He said He would send His Spirit. He told His apostles and disciples to wait for the Spirit. We see the dove, the sign of the Spirit of God descending upon Christ at His baptism and at the same time we hear the Father's voice (Matthew 17:5). This is an instance of the presence of all three Persons of God at one time. In the Old Testament there are instances when the Spirit descends while God's voice is heard, some while "One like the Son of Man" is present, sometimes without any physical presence. With all these references, with all these interchangeable personages intertwined, how can one not believe that they are One and the same despite their differentness? A divine mystery, yes. My point is that it is acceptable for one to feel that one understands God's character, and, more importantly, that one accepts God as God. It's faith that trusts what it doesn't fully comprehend—or perhaps doesn't exactly comprehend, but merely accepts instead. It's a soulish understanding; it's a knowing that it's okay no matter *what* it is because it's of God and everything that's of God is perfect, holy—and just fine.

Through adolescence and puberty I moved through a few different schools in and out of Catholic situations, but in the long run ended up in a better situation, for I ended up in "catechism" class for a while with our parish priest, Father O'Donnell, who was more like a beloved uncle than some unapproachable authority figure as indeed some of the figures in the Catholic school setting were. When I had questions, he allowed me to wonder and ask, and he provided an environment that not only allowed, but encouraged, discussion. In fact, he gave me credit for having a thinking mind, making statements such as, "I know *you* know this one—" although, truthfully at times he caught me out, for sometimes I really didn't know the things he thought I did.

Because I grew up in church, those in the church were like my extended family; I was comfortable there. This was good in many ways but eventually it gave way to something very bad, because I began to see the nature of the deep hypocrisy that could be present in churches—and in the world overall. Unfortunately, no one thinks to hide things from children when they are young, and the old adage "little pitchers have big ears" is true. Children see and hear things they should not and they are watching what their elders do. It was still the era of "children should be seen and not heard." It never occurred to anyone that the things they were doing would impact our young lives—that we could see that what some of the parishioners were doing did not line up with the Word that our good priest was giving us from the pulpit and teaching us in the rectory (priest's residence) and in our home where he came often as a guest.

Thus when my adolescent blood rose—as was inevitable—and rebellion began, it was against this church family who I turned as well. I missed our dear priest, for he had been reassigned away from us before I quit church so it was not as if I walked away from him. I wonder now if I would have sought him out if he had remained there in the parish—whether in my turmoil I would have gone to him for help and comfort. But I can only wonder, for he was gone.

As the things of God are pure and holy and found by diligently seeking Him, so do we only remain in the Spirit through pursuing God. In my childish way, even as I rebelled during that tumultuous time, I still had a tenderness in my heart for God, thorny though that heart was fast becoming. When I rebelled, I missed being with God and sometimes went looking for Him, wanting to be in His presence. Occasionally I would go to a more modern church downtown, seeking a service that was different, a different place where I might be comfortable, because I couldn't go back to my old church. It wasn't home any more. Our priest was gone and the church itself was on the verge of being closed down temporarily so it could be refurbished and turned into a historic site. The congregation was scattering and I belonged nowhere; I had no spiritual home. I was adrift.

As the timidity of my childhood morphed into the awkwardness of the teen years, my soul and my spirit screamed for some sort of outlet. I was a prolific poet and that was at least some sort of channel. Looking back now at some of the verses, I can read my soul's cry. I seldom felt well for I was plagued by allergies and the medicine I took usually kept me feeling groggy, so I slogged through my days with little interest. My mother was usually exasperated with me, and I felt intimidated by the fact that I followed on the heels of my smart, vivacious sister. My music and art helped some, but even in these I had only a little self-confidence.

I attended a "new Mass" and the simple language and modern music touched me deep inside. It felt like a coming-home to me. I tried to talk to my mother about it because I had felt the presence of the LORD so strongly. But my mother thought it was weird and decided that I was being unduly influenced by some strange force that she was uncomfortable with. Instead of continuing in the all-girls Catholic high school I attended, I was pulled out and thrust into public school for my two final years of high school. For this I was unprepared in every way.

Inexperienced socially and often feeling awkward, I mostly kept to myself. In the Catholic girls' school I had left, things had been much easier. We wore uniforms so fashion was not an issue, there were no boys to deal with, and our studies kept us so busy there was little time to be distracted—and indeed little to distract us even if we *had* had the time. The only thing that was positive about the public school was that I was so far ahead in my studies that I could basically coast through the last two years of school, which was good since, with the grogginess from allergy meds, the social bewilderment, the resentment at being plopped into a new environment and the usual teen angst, I was ripe for rebellion. I began to wander off task and into mischief, mild though it was at the first.

My one "salvation" at the time was that I had learned at fourteen that I could write. Words flowed from me with ease and grace. It was nothing I had learned; I recognized that it was a gift and my gift was obvious to others as well. I was published the first time at the age of fifteen in a neighborhood newspaper. I was an artist as well; I understood line, form and color. My art teachers encouraged me and special training followed in the form of summer scholarships to Minneapolis art institutes. I found others like myself in due course and immersed myself in their world. I shuffled between the literary magazine workroom and the art room in my spare time—which I had plenty of. Who cared if others thought me weird? Alas, this world apart only caused more tension at home. These, my new friends, were odd, "square pegs." Yet, ever curious, I set out to learn them and in the process to perhaps learn myself.

I met a kid who taught me things I'd never heard before. I was drawn to him and to the things he told me. He taught me to embrace new ideas, to be "open-minded." He showed me his "bible," the satanic bible. This book taught that things such as hatred are good, for it purges your spirit. Theft is good, for you are entitled to anything your enterprise can get you. Hurt those who would stop you. Even murder could be considered an asset. The antithesis of everything God says—that is the satanic bible.

The most appalling thing about this book is that I was not appalled. Instead I was intrigued. I got a copy of this book through this boy and studied it. Parents, pay attention to what your children are studying and reading in their leisure time and what is going on in their spiritual lives in addition to or instead of church (See *Appendix III: Paganism in Our Homes*). Don't allow them to say that certain books and programs are "innocent," for they are decidedly *not*. Make your children accountable. Know what is in their rooms and among their books and music; keep everything open for discussion. Nip wrong in the bud and take them before God before satanic practices can gain a foothold in their lives. In the Old Testament, they would have been executed. As their parents, if you had not stopped them, you would have been executed as well. Do not ignore or pass over their wrongdoing and think of it as innocent and passing recreation that they will grow out of. It is the sin of idolatry and witchcraft and very dangerous.

But God does not let His sheep go easily. I could try to blame my parents for switching me from school to school, for indeed I moved through seven schools in elementary through senior high school. But life is what it is and I will instead point out the very positive things in my life: the good, warm home, food and clothes; growing up in church; good education; discipline; humor and love. The final analysis is always the same: our lives are what they are and what we make of them. We take what we get and we are responsible for what we do with what we are given.

As I skipped about in high school I developed a certain arrogance, for I realized I could talk my way around my teachers, around my absences from classes. I could generally show up, take a test, write a paper, or do a presentation and come out at least reasonably well.

Yet in all these things, God was somewhere in me. The seeds of faith had been sown in me early. They were there and, if not lying exactly dormant, at least they were safe and warm and sometimes watered, sometimes weeded a little, sometimes fed and nurtured, even if I had no idea about what was going on. God can work in us even when we don't even know He's there.

I met a nice boy, a protestant. Inside me was a seed of faith. In quiet times when I wasn't cultivating my strangeness (for this was indeed deliberate) and investigating satanism, I *did* consider God. ("I will bless the LORD Who has counseled me; indeed my mind instructs me in the night .

. ." Psalm 16:7) This nice boyfriend didn't like the things I was into, and said so. He was not an angel, but really not a bad kid either. He tried to turn me around, but I was headed down a different path than he was. I wanted to experiment and he wanted to observe what he knew to be right rather than wrong. I had early gained access to God by what seemed to be an innate faith and God had embedded within me a deep need for Him. It had indeed taken root, but that's not where I was headed then. Maybe this boy prayed for me. I don't know. I do know some people did, especially a certain couple aunties and a certain neighbor, for they told me so.

I never thought of resisting going to church with my family, although resistance would have been futile and would have only caused clamor—and I hated strife. When I later worked Sundays and missed church I sometimes went of my own will, and it felt good being there. But my spirit—such an active spirit!—was ever in turmoil. Always in that young spirit there was such a tugging, such a pulling, a pushing, a tearing, a rending. Such pain, even, so very deep within me. I can even feel it now, thinking back. If one will reflect, it is this same psyche at war, this same "angst," such torment and anxiety within each prepubescent/adolescent emerging soul as he or she reaches the "age of reason" and becomes accountable for his or her own soul's condition or estate. I have seen over and over how much more fortunate those are who commit to Jesus at a young age and hang onto Him through the rocky teen years. They emerge much more triumphantly as a whole person—and if not exactly victoriously, certainly in much better shape than those of us who go through without Him. What an answer Jesus is! How I wish I could have gone through with Him, knowing Him as I do now. They say that if you can get a kid to Jesus before he or she is 12 years old, they are more than likely a lifelong Christian. I like to think that's true, because all my grandchildren have made their decisions for Christ already. I pray that it is so, because I like to think of them as having a much easier time of their teen years than I had. Yet I know of so many who made early decisions that didn't have an easier time despite those decisions. Ah, faith—here is where it comes in again. I just have to have faith for my grandkids, that they'll come safely through, that they'll have that easier, gentler time because of Jesus in them.

At home I found no rest. My father was a man of a great but quiet faith. I suppose it never occurred to him that his children might not naturally come to that same faith. He was also a man who greatly loved children, but didn't know what to do with those same children when they reached adolescence and then their teen years. My mother was always busy and stressed, with six kids and a job. When home should have been a haven, I only wanted to be away from it, but I suppose this is nothing new as most teenagers begin seeking to pull away toward freedom. It seemed that I was always at odds with my parents; I felt I could never please. In fact, in my last two quarters of my senior year in high school, I was more often grounded (on restriction) than not, which compounded the problem of tension between us. I realize that my parents' idea was to keep me home where they could monitor my behavior, as I did the same with my own son, but I only became more angry—and brooded.

If only children and adolescents could understand the reason for discipline. Can we though, even as adults, see and understand God's discipline of us? Do we recognize it when it comes? When we are hurting, we need to wait and pray and trust God that, in faith, He will bring us through.

I have heard people say that they can not love God as a father because their earthly father was too stern, or harsh or even cruel, but I think this is only an excuse. Though I was angered by what I considered to be my parents' over-strictness, I never felt affected by my relationship with them compared to my relationship with God. I have a faith-based love for God, which in no way is impeded or blocked by anything experienced between what my earthly parents and I went through, for this love for my heavenly Father was planted—*embedded*—long before that faith in my earthly parents was so wounded. I also underwent a "time of forgiveness" as the prophet said in Proverbs ("a time for every purpose under heaven") in my church many years later when I could compare my pain with the pain I inflicted on my Savior for which He suffered and died, by which He paid for my many, many sins. When I compare these sorrows with what anyone on this earth has caused me, it is nothing compared to that and thus easily forgivable—fleeting, temporary, as *nothing* compared to the anguish I caused my Savior with my faithless, sinful ways. Thus, what I perceived as the suffering my earthly parents caused me, especially being unaware of it, is easily forgiven. Yes, it took some time, but understanding what we forgive as opposed to what Christ not only has forgiven us but continues to forgive us every day—well, it keeps things in perspective. We need to do that—keep things in perspective—and to keep short accounts not only by making sure we confess our sins to one another and to Christ frequently, but by making sure we deal with our anger and forgive others freely as well.

Parents, be very careful with your children, not to provoke them to anger. Having been so hurt down through the years and then having hurt my own son, I know whereof I speak. The Word of God warns us, "Fathers, do not provoke your children to anger, but bring them up in the discipline and instruction of the LORD" (Ephesians 6:4).

All of these things together—these hurts, these pullings, these trials and errors, these searchings, all contributed to my dance with the enemy. Stupid, yes. But youth has never been noted for its wisdom. What they caused in me was a rashness and a restlessness that caused me to want to flee; I was in search of a peace I could not find inside. There was so much hurt in me that I could not "grow where I was planted," could not flourish where I was.

Thus I began pursuing my independence at the age of sixteen. I was, I was certain, able to make it on my own through subsistence living. I didn't care that I wouldn't have a TV, stereo, piano, laundry. I would have food from my waitress job, bus service, hitchhiking (I refused to consider how dangerous *that* could be!) and my feet to get me around, the public library for entertainment, and blissfully, my own space. Peace. Quiet. Privacy. I could wash my laundry in the bathtub. (Who cared if I had to share a bathroom? I shared one at home with seven other people, didn't I?) I didn't care about these things. I wished, simply, to be alone, to pursue my writing and my art. I knew somehow that I could make it. My basic nature today is not so different—I am a loner still, I still like my solitude and I still like things simple and basic.

I rented a room where I knew I couldn't get my money back, thinking that would clinch the deal. But I didn't know my mother well enough. She marched me back downtown and threatened the landlady with arrest for dealing with a minor. She got my money back and I was taken back home before I ever got to live in my little room. I guess I shouldn't have told her about it. Since that didn't work out and I still wanted to get away, I tried again. I ran away soon after to a friend's sister's apartment and called my mother and told her I wasn't coming home until she met certain conditions.

She refused, but I went home anyway. As badly as I wanted out, I had in me the seeds of faith that made me conform to God's basic commands, one of which was to honor my parents. As badly as I wanted to rebel, open rebellion was not yet fully blown within me.

One thing that helped fasten me to God for a while was that I loved music and it had the ability to touch me deep inside. I sang in the children's choir, and when I became a teen I moved to the adult choir. That time of music had the power to stir my soul, to lead me into worship, and to periodically renew in me my relationship with God. Even as I was rebelling, even though I had a foolish young heart, still God had a strong hold on me and was able to touch my spirit. Especially poignant and heartrendingly tender for me was Easter time and the time of remembrance of the passion and death of Christ when I pondered Christ's suffering. The Catholic church, so rich in tradition, ritual, and rite touched the chords of devotion in my young spirit and to some extent renewed me even in my still unsaved condition. When I contemplated Christ's death, even though I did not yet fully understand that His death was for *my own sin,* I was pulled into God's sphere and touched by His infinite compassion. There is still no time for me like this annual time of remembrance of His passion and death, especially now that I more fully understand the implication of these events, and their meaning for my own soul in eternity.

Despite these periods of renewal, finally at seventeen I met my first husband. When he proposed to me two weeks after we met, I was so flattered and infatuated that I could not see beyond it and accepted without reservation. I had so little self-esteem that I couldn't believe this handsome man would want me—*me!* My mother, however, was horrified, aghast. She begged me not to marry him, for as a mature adult, she could better read his character. All I could think about was my dream of having my own home, and being married seemed the easy way to get there. My mother and I had a bitter fight on my eighteenth birthday and I moved out of the house the next day. She begged me to stay, saying she would do anything. But I was young and in love, and love, as Shakespeare said, is blind. We were married one week later. Although my parents vowed they wouldn't come to the wedding, they did anyway. They truly did love me; they truly only wanted the best for me. We were a strong family unit. They wanted only to rescue me from this sad mistake, for I had only known the man five weeks.

Alas, it was out of the frying pan and into the fire. Where I had thought to find peace there was none. There was in fact even greater turmoil than I had ever before experienced, for I had married a clinically insane sociopath who abused me in ways I'd never imagined. I was young and so naïve. He insisted I work full-time, cook everything from scratch, and do all the housekeeping and laundry to absolute perfection and then wanted me to sell drugs to supplement my income. *He* didn't feel the need to do anything for, he told me, that was why he was married. Every penny had to be accounted for and I was not allowed to speak to anyone, lest I tell someone of what went on in the house. I was sent to the store and timed; woe be unto me if there was a long line at the checkout or if the price was raised on something, for I would not return on time or with the change expected (supermarkets often did not provide sales receipts in those days). There is a great deal more to these torments that I could tell, but it does not help anything to relate them, so I will let it go and just say that I know that God protected me through my life with this man. Suffice it to say that it was brutal physically, mentally, psychologically, emotionally and even spiritually. I was battered and tortured viciously and repeatedly, and could have been killed a number of times. But I will not go into this further, for God rescued me. This is just another path that I walked on my journey toward God. I was seeking God even then, though I didn't realize it myself.

My husband wanted a family, but he wanted other things as well that were not compatible with family. He wanted rock concerts and drunken, drug-filled revels and those sorts of things. However, in order to get closer to family life, we began to go to church. The church we were lured into was a cult and not a Christian church at all. The strangest thing about this church is that they strongly believe that if one is "chosen," one will have a vision. So, of course, everyone has a "vision." The advantage of becoming a member? You don't get to go to heaven—that is only for a very few elect. You instead get to go to some sort of paradise, a place apart. So what's the point? They're very family oriented; family is the salvation. Later, when being married meant mostly taking my life and my unborn child's life into my hands, I escaped with the help of a neighbor (literally being hidden by her, then having her speed away with me in the car when he wasn't looking). I was pregnant at the time and he had kicked me down two flights of stairs. I very naturally went and asked "my" church for help. However, this supposedly family-oriented church would not help me, even though I was a member, unless I could work full-time for them, despite being sick. One position was to take care of 7 children and do the housework for the mother, expecting her eighth child. Since I was ill and told them that was too strenuous, I was offered instead a position working in the church office 30–40 hours a week in exchange for room and board. I didn't even have bus fare to get to the church.

When I repeated that I was sick and could scarcely hold food down and had to drag myself out of bed and would be glad to work when I was better, I was told, "We don't work that way." So much for that faithless church. I can't help but wonder who their God is.

It is sad but not surprising that I did not meet Jesus Christ in that church. As far as I know, my first husband never met Jesus Christ at all. He lost his life in a motorcycle accident when he was 21 years old, and our son was only 8 months old. Our son never knew him, for despite my best tries, I was never able to live with him more than a few weeks at a time, for he continued to torment me. The final straw came when he threatened our 5-month-old baby too; I moved out then as soon as he left for work, and went into hiding again. This time I told no one where I was going; it was the only way to be safe.

I sometimes think about this time, and think that maybe God rescued me from this man by his death, for while he was alive he kept finding me wherever I was hiding, and attacking me. But this is a horrible thought, for then I wonder if he is in hell. But maybe, says my faith within me, *maybe* he met Christ somewhere along the way and at that last minute, at that last second, he remembered Him and cried out to God, and God poured out His mercy and grace on him and he went to heaven.

After all this, my parents tried to take me back into their home, but I couldn't do it. I needed the peace of my aloneness. I needed to be a family with my son. I needed my solitude. I also had my spirit to attend to. I had met some people and they were leading me spiritually—but down the old evil path again. They responded to the strong spiritual currents within me and groomed me in the satanic arts. I fell in with witches, some of whom I trusted because they professed to be "white" or "good" witches. Two of these were church-going women of a large supposedly Christian denomination. They recognized my potential, and began to teach me and use me. I suppose that for a while I was as a pet; I was young and a novelty, with a bright mind and eager spirit. I was willing to learn and had an excellent memory and a pliable spirit. I imagine it was good for their egos to have such a willing student.

But they began to sap my intellectual and psychic strength and I soon began to feel the drain on my spirit. I felt again the need to get away on my own. I lived with two of my mentors, and when one moved out, it was easier for me to see that I needed to get away from the other one too. Soon after she moved as well, and I was free and moved off by myself with my baby son. I think back now and wonder what sorts of influence these things I was doing had on his tender infant spirit, whether such demonic things may have attached themselves to him.

Still the good seeds of faith planted deep within me had not been torn out or choked by the evil weeds of the spiritual wickedness I was cultivating in my soul. As this evil spiritual power grew, I still had no true concept of what I was doing or of how truly dangerous this was. I was intrigued, but to me it was more of a hobby born of rebellion and anger, and a fascination with the spiritual world. I was an artist, a bohemian. I was a counterculturist and living a hippie life style, and I did not see anything wrong in what I was doing. I felt a power in it that I did not fully understand. I did not question that there *was* power in it; that I *did* understand.

Although I pursued occultic practices, I still pursued God at the same time. I met a woman of another cultish "faith" and began to meet with her once a week for a few months, but before very long her answers to my questions didn't ring true. She couldn't satisfy my longing for a relationship with God. She couldn't guarantee me a true salvation; she couldn't bring me the peace I so desperately craved. What did she have for me? I tried to tell her I was no longer interested, but she was tenacious, persistent in her determination to convert me. She would not stop coming. I could not get rid of her. I finally lied to her. I was moving away, I said. Where? I was moving to Canada, and I didn't have an address for her, I said. I'd send a postcard when I got there. Finally she stopped coming.

It *seemed* as though eventually I stumbled through and found God simply by trial and error. The *truth,* however, is that God orchestrated it all. He kept me safe through what could have been death through illness, alcohol and drug overdose, stupid and careless accidents, being in dangerous situations—in the wrong place at the wrong time. But God ordered my steps because He had His hand on me all the time. He planted seeds of faith deep inside me before I was born. He watered them with my innocent tears when I was a small child, when I was a tortured teen, when I was lost and had no one to point the way, and when I didn't even know enough to call on Him. He kept me safe because my name was written in the Lamb's Book of Life (Revelation 3:5) and He didn't want it erased. He saved me because He loves me and He has a plan for my life. He kept me safe across many rocky paths, through many stormy gales because He loves and cherishes me. He did it all before I even knew what faith was. Then He brought me to a point of faith because of one tiny seed of faith that had taken hold before I even knew what faith was.

Then He answered me at my point of need and has never let me go.

A Faith of Sorts

"See to it that no one takes you captive through philosophy and empty deception, according to the tradition of men, according to the elementary principles of the world, rather than according to Christ."
—*Colossians 2:8–9*

When my husband George and I were first married, we bought an old house in Grand Rapids, Michigan where we soon became part of the neighborhood. Almost immediately, the neighbors a few doors down invited us to church. Although George and I had both been raised in church we were both more than disinterested—we were against involvement in "religion," considering it a waste of our time. What I didn't realize at the time was that my belief system and our way of life were a religion of our own, and that I was paying dearly for rejecting the things of God. My son Kirk was just starting school and was a very social little person, and he wanted to go to church. Being a liberal in all things and not wanting to impede his young development, I agreed. So I sat little Kirk out on the front step on Sunday mornings and watched from behind the curtains till they came, so he could go with the neighbors. I had no reason to refuse to allow it when he appeared to want to go so much. He returned home each week longing for Mommy and Daddy to join him and go to this neat place where everyone was so nice to him. And each week, I steadfastly refused.

My life, whether I would have honestly acknowledged it at the time or not, was becoming increasingly unsatisfactory. I was a substance abuser and had no real aims or goals. I had the hazy notion of wanting to be "happy" as everyone does, but had no notion of how to pursue this. I was a writer and an artist, and though my writing was prolific I did not right then have an outlet and I was getting a little tired of rejection slips, which are accepted as a matter of course by most writers. My dissatisfaction with my life grew, and a restlessness within me took root.

Although I loved my husband and should have been "happy," my life began to crumble. I was alone much of the time, since my husband traveled. This was an ideal life for a writer, but I was often very sick. I began having terrible stomach problems that caused a degree of debilitation and a great deal of pain. When I reached the end of my strength, one night I cried out the simple prayer, "God, if You're really there, do something!"

He did. I fell asleep shortly after praying that simple prayer, and slept soundly. The next day, Saturday, I experienced an overwhelming need, an actual *urgency* to attend church that Sunday. When George returned home from out of town that afternoon (the family business as carpenters caused George and his father and two brothers to travel often), I told him about all this and he shrugged and agreed. He has always been easygoing and agreeable in most matters. However, the next morning he did not want to get up.

"We can go next week," he said.

But I insisted and persevered, and got us all together for the trip that Sunday morning. I don't recall what I said to Kirk's Christian friends when I told them he wouldn't be going with them, but I can now, as a Christian hoping for others to know God, imagine the delight they felt that morning.

When we got to the family church, Calvary Baptist of Grand Rapids, Michigan, (George's uncle, John White, was then pastor), I began to have terrible pains in my stomach, to double up with cramps and to feel quite faint. I began perspiring profusely and shaking, and also having a kind of spell which I now know to be a seizure, and George said, "OK, we're going home."

Now here's faith. I turned to George and said, "Oh, no. God's not going to let me be sick my first day back at church." I remember this moment as clearly and vividly as though it was only yesterday.

Where did that kind of faith come from in someone who apparently didn't even know God? Was that a seed of something God had planted in me when He created me, when He foreknew me before I was formed in my mother's womb, when He knew me before I was even born?

The Word of God says so: "For those whom He *foreknew*, He also predestined to become conformed to the image of His Son . . ." (Romans 8:29).

In other words, God meant for me to know Him from the time He created me. Apparently I had stronger feelings about God than I knew at that time.

We attended church without further incident and, while I do not remember the sermon, I do remember the singing. "Holy, holy, holy, LORD God Almighty . . ." It was an old hymn, one I remembered from my childhood.

I filled out a little visitor's card, not to make a statement or declaration of any sort, but to request a visit from someone at the church. I don't remember thinking much about this, only that it was the thing for me to do just then.

Some fellows from the church came calling the following Tuesday. They asked whether I expected to go to heaven, then shot down my reasons for thinking I would, one by one. I was a good person, I said. (Yeah, right. I had a filthy, cursing mouth, freely hated people, considered anything I did was fine as long as I could get away with it.) But I had been baptized, I argued. Again not good enough.

Finally, in tears, I yelped, "Well what am I going to do?"

Gently they explained that I couldn't earn my way into heaven by what I did, but that it was a gift from God that He gave freely to anyone who received Christ. I had believed since childhood that Christ had lived and died, even "for sins," but I had never understood that Jesus had chosen to die for *me* personally. In fact, if I had been the only person who had ever lived, God's love is so great that Jesus still would have done it all, just for me alone. When I understood that I had only to sincerely desire God's forgiveness and then commit myself to Him, I freely received that gift of salvation. I did not understand until that day that in all the years I had been growing up in church I had not learned that I needed a living relationship with God—a relationship that made Him a more personal God to me, that made Him real to me. Jesus did not just die "for sins" but for me, *for my own sins.* I had to understand that His sacrifice was something that I needed as a ransom for me personally—that I personally needed someone to step in for me, to pay the death penalty that I had hanging over my head.

I received bad news and good that day: the bad news was that I couldn't go to heaven under my own steam. I was unworthy and could never earn my way in. The good news was that God had made a way for the price to be paid for my sins, and Jesus was that price. I had only to accept this payment, to ask Jesus to be my substitute, my redemption. He had already paid in my place. When I understood, when I grasped the truth of what they were telling me, I embraced it with all my might. These good men explained to me how I must humble myself, ask forgiveness from Jesus for my sins, and accept His free gift of love and forgiveness. Simple enough to do, and so I did just that.

A sense of peace replaced my agitation, and I felt as though an interminable, everlasting, wearying burden had been lifted from my shoulders. It was a truly physical feeling beyond the spiritual cleansing I received, accompanied by an emotional and psychological change as well. I am not saying that one who makes this commitment necessarily "feels" something, for it is by faith that we are saved. Don't wait for a feeling, for you may not have one. Believe it by faith. (See *How to Become a Christian.*)

All of this happened scarcely eighteen months after an enraged junkie had taken aim with a shotgun and fired directly at my head from not six feet away—and missed. That event was a strange one—so near death, yet at the time I had been filled with some strange bravado that told me I wasn't scheduled to die just then. I'd faced death from illnesses and beatings before that, too, and I was still here on earth. I'd just never felt like I was going to die. I just didn't feel ready. Believe me, I wasn't. I was a model of wickedness, the product of a depraved mind, a slave to sin, liar, drunkard, curser of God, malicious and evil. I wonder that God left me to walk the earth, other than that He loved me (Yes! Even then!) and had a plan for my life. God numbers our days and chooses when we die. Fortunately, He leaves us every chance to choose Him. Joyfully, He saved me alive for that one day so I might choose Him, so I might have that chance.

That day I had the faith to believe in Christ and I began a new life. Before that day, people had been praying for me. Shortly before I had come to that day, I had been a neighbor to the man who shot at me, as well as to a young woman who told me repeatedly that I needed Jesus Christ in my life—and that no matter what I thought, I was not happy because I did not have Jesus. Her presence in my life and her prayers for me may very well have been what kept me alive. There is a lesson we can learn in that. We must be diligent to pray for and minister to those that God puts in our path, for we never know what may be facing them, nor how close they may be to eternity without our prayers. After moving from that place, we lived briefly in a neighborhood in another state where an elderly man offered me and my son a ride for a few blocks, and then told me that Jesus loved me and had a plan for me. Within a year, Jesus claimed me as His own.

There is faith all around us, but faith is not enough. Faith misplaced is just hollow confidence. I have heard people say, "Yes, but he (or she) really believes it," as though faith in a false doctrine will save someone. I had this kind of a faith in me at one time, but faith in and of itself is not the answer. Just because I believe it will rain lemonade at 2:00 doesn't make it so. Just because someone is sincere in their belief that a certain sect and/or their works will take them to heaven doesn't make it so.

God made this very clear. "' … this people draw near with their words and honor Me with their lip service, but they remove their hearts far from Me, and their reverence for Me consists of tradition learned [by rote] . . ." (Isaiah 29:13).

In my "BC days" ("before Christ"), my life was made up of faith in myself, on a foundation of what I felt George and I could build in our lives together for our family and for our future. The Word of God tells us that if any man builds on any foundation other than Christ, it is in vain. Even if one does meet Jesus at some point then goes on to try to live as before instead of turning his or her life fully over to Christ, it is still in vain. Perhaps such a one may be saved, but that is only for God to know (I Corinthians 3:14–15). It is a gamble with one's soul, a gamble with eternity. Why live such a faithless life, devoid of peace when God can give such a life of serenity and quietude, such joy and fulfillment to those who turn fully to Him? It is so much easier to come to Jesus and lay it all down, to give one's life fully to Him.

I have recently spent twenty years in the "Bible Belt" and have met more misguided so-called "Christians" than I ever knew existed. If America is the "Christian nation" she is so reputed to be, then the south is the Baptist region. I have heard so much of "born-a-Baptist-die-a-Baptist," "once-saved-always-saved" people that I could just cry. I have found these people the hardest people I've ever met to witness to because they sincerely believe that they have a relationship with God yet, for the most part, they know nothing about Him and worse yet, they care to know nothing about Him.

The Word of God says, "Unless a man be born anew . . ." (John 3:3)—this indicates a fresh start, a renewal. Indeed the word "repentance" indicates not only remorse, sorrow, regret, but true humility and a fresh start, a "turning." Thus, if one is "born again," as Christ directs in the Scriptures, it means more than the overworked term of "saved." Let us then be "born again" and renew ourselves and go on from there to "work out our salvation with fear and trembling" (Philippians 2:12) day by day. This means to continue steadfastly to walk with Christ with every intention of doing whatever one can to make one's life a godly example fit for the label of "Christian." One must prove one's salvation by what he or she does. Words are easy. A doctor who does not heal may as well never call himself one. A Christian who shows no evidence of being one should never bother calling himself one, and indeed leads others astray and shames Christ by calling himself by that name.

The Bible says that those who love God must hate evil—there is no other way ("Hate evil, you who love the LORD, Who preserves the souls of His godly ones; He delivers them from the hand of the wicked" (Psalm 97:10).) The Word further says, "They profess to know God, but by their deeds they deny Him, being detestable and disobedient and worthless for any good deed" (Titus 1:16).

But these so-called Christians who are not really Christians at all have a different way of thinking. They have faith in their faith. Some of them have what is referred to as "fire insurance," although many have not even that. In other words, they believe they are saved from hell's fire (hence the "insurance"), but they have no evidence of it in their lives. Perhaps their faith in their salvation is enough, but I don't find evidence of this in the Scriptures. Perhaps they are continually repentant—perhaps they continually beg God on their beds at night to save them in spite of themselves—we cannot know.

When we stand before God at the end of time to be judged, each of us will be asked to defend ourselves for our crimes (sins), just as we stand in a court of law before a judge. Unless we have an attorney (Christ), we have no defender. If Christ stands with us and answers for us, we are forgiven. But we must "retain" Him, our "attorney," beforehand; we must receive Him, make Him part of our lives before that Judgment Day. If we belong to Jesus, if He is to be with us on that day, if He is our Savior, we need not be afraid, for He will stand with us. He will bring us forward before the Father and say, "Come you who are blessed by My Father; take your inheritance, the kingdom prepared for you . . ." (Matthew 25:21)

I wish to know that I will come before Jesus, be clasped in His embrace, be brought by Him before the Father, be called His very own, and be welcomed to His table for the Lamb's feast, and walk with Him in eternity. I don't want to show up afraid of what Jesus will say about me, trembling in fear of eternal damnation, wondering what my end will be. Instead, I want to look forward to being with my King and my Father forever.

However, to those who wonder whether they are saved I say, "If you are saved, show me by the way you live." The Word of God is abundantly clear on this: " ... show me your faith without the works, and I will show you *my* faith *by* my works" (James 2:18).

In other words, if you really believe in God, prove it to me by what you do. Just because someone believes in God doesn't mean they're saved: "You believe that God is one. You do well; the demons also believe, and shudder" (James 2:19).

A man I know used to have occasional dreams that people had been "raptured" (taken up bodily into heaven *en masse,* as one in a body together (I Thessalonians 5:16–17)), and whenever he had this dream he would call me to see if I was still around, because he believed if I was, then the event had not yet happened.

"I was worried," he'd say. "But I knew if you were still around it hadn't happened."

He's stopped calling about these dreams, but I don't know if that means he's stopped having them. He also used to express to me concern that he'd committed the "unpardonable sin" which means to "blaspheme the Holy Spirit." In lay terms, this means to reject God so completely and totally as to leave no question as to one's heart—that there was so much contempt for God there was no question of ever accepting Him. I used to tell him that, if this was a concern to him, then he had not committed this sin. This question has also stopped. I have recently heard that this man is an alcoholic, is gambling heavily and dealing drugs, so I don't have to think too deeply about why these questions have stopped. The last few times I have tried to talk to him about the LORD, I have been met with either stony silence, with snide remarks, or with rude comments. As for myself, I don't mind how he talks to me; for I delight in bearing such for my LORD, but neither do I wish to waste the precious words of God on someone with so little regard for the things of the LORD or the precious Name of Jesus.

But I am acutely aware of what is said in Isaiah 41:11, "All who rage against You [God] will surely be ashamed and disgraced; those who oppose You will be as nothing and perish."

Oh that I could spare him that! I'm sorely afraid that the questions have stopped because this man doesn't want to hear the answers anymore—that he wants to avoid the subject altogether because he knows the answer, and it is not in his favor. There is nothing more I can do but pray. I can certainly no longer witness to him, for he doesn't want to hear it. There are even times now when I feel that perhaps God doesn't even want me to pray for this one, so then I pray that God will send someone that he will listen to. I love him still, I cherish him. I weep at the thought of him lost for eternity.

The problem is that this man was saved as a youth, was

full of God's Spirit, and dedicated to the LORD. The Scriptures speak of this situation and I have seen it borne out not only in this man's life but in other's lives.

"It is impossible for those who have once been enlightened, who have once tasted the heavenly gift, who have shared in the Holy Spirit, who have tasted the goodness of the Word of God and the powers of the coming age, *if they fall away,* to be brought back to repentance, because to their loss they are crucifying the Son of God all over again and subjecting Him to public disgrace" (Hebrews 6:4–6). This is what "blasphemy against the Holy Spirit" truly means.

The problem in this case is that he may well be aware of what he has turned his back on, what he has walked away from, Who he has hardened his heart towards, what he has chosen to give up. But I do not know this; I cannot know this. Are his mind and spirit so blocked by the enemy that he cannot see and understand what is happening? Does God make special provision for such as him because people around him who love him have faith for him? He has publicly shamed Christ by refusing Him. And yet, I have faith that there are miracles—that he may still turn back and beg God's forgiveness. By some miracle, it could yet happen that he could return to Christ. That's the type of faith I have to have. I must not let go of that.

I try to pray for him but it's almost as if I feel in my spirit that it's too late and I can't discern if I'm angry for the Lord's sake, if the LORD is telling me to leave it be (Mark 6:11)—or whether I've just given up. The only thing I can do is leave him in God's hands—again, in faith. Perhaps God has someone prepared to come after me that this man *will* listen to. Just to think about it hurts and makes me so sad. How could he not want Christ, Who loves him so tenderly? How could anyone not want Christ? Those of us who do know and love Christ are faced with this all the time. We can't understand how anyone could not want Jesus.

But this man has some type of faith. He thinks he's okay with God, although he never prays, never attends church (not that church attendance makes a Christian), never relies on God for anything, and curses God's name instead of praising it. He even flatly refuses to take his children to church, even refuses to drop them off. He says he will give his children anything, but he will not give them this. He believes (or still did at one time) he has a place in heaven (although why he'd want to be with God eternally when God is the furthest thing from his mind, I cannot tell) because he once made a commitment to God. He has this strange sort of faith, though what he bases it on, I do not know, for he denies God in every way.

II Timothy 3:2–5 says that these are "lovers of self, lovers of money, boastful, proud, abusive, disobedient to their parents, ungrateful, unholy, without love, unforgiving, slanderous, without self-control, brutal, not lovers of good, treacherous, rash, conceited, lovers of pleasure rather than lovers of God—having a form of faith but denying its power."

What I do know is that he believes that the Bible says no one can take away someone's salvation. He is right; no one can take your salvation away from you. However, anyone and everyone is free to park their salvation by the wayside and walk away from it—and many do just that. He apparently has. Yes, the Bible says we are not to judge others or to condemn them (Luke 6:37), but that's not what I'm doing. I am simply observing his life and telling what I observe. A person who has no relationship with God cannot reasonably expect to call himself God's and to turn up at the gates of heaven seeking admission when he gets there.

Jesus will say to these, "Truly I say to you, I do not know you" (Matthew 25:12).

The Bible addresses this issue by asking whether one can accept salvation through faith then consider this gift as an excuse to continue in sin ("What shall we say then? Are we to continue in sin so that grace may increase? May it never be! How shall we who died to sin still live in it?" (Romans 6:1–2)). The answer, of course, is "no," for if one is truly dead to sin, one cannot still live in sin, for that is contrary to the new nature. ("Everyone who names the name of the Lord is to abstain from wickedness" (II Timothy 2:19).)

One is either redeemed—"saved"—and dead to the sin nature, or not truly redeemed at all. There is no room within the soul for both natures. One nature must be abandoned. This is not to say that one ceases to sin but that the nature is changed and sin is avoided rather than followed. A striving after holiness follows a true conversion experience. Just as the result of one's continual sinning in the old nature is eternal loss, the result of continual renewal in Christ in the new nature results in joy, peace, redemption, and eternal life.

Again, as regards those who seek to enter the kingdom, upon meeting Jesus, He plainly tells us, "'Not everyone who calls out "Lord, Lord" will enter the kingdom of heaven, but only those who do what My Father in heaven wants them to do. ... on Judgment Day I will say to them , "Get away from Me, I never knew you!"'" (Matthew 7:22–23)

The Word clearly says in II Chronicles 15:2, "The Lord is with you when you are with Him ... but if you forsake Him He will forsake you." Period.

It is true that it is by faith alone that we are saved. But something must prove that our faith is real, that it is founded on something. God wants us, and He gives us every opportunity to turn back from sin and return to Him. He is patient and longsuffering. He will continue to pursue us, but there comes a point when He will stop calling us back. If we live in an ungodly manner and turn away from God's ways, He will not everlastingly trail after us calling out to us, begging us to turn away from those ways and come back to Him. He will turn away just as we do. Make no mistake about it: if you live a life apart from God and the way He asks you to live it and you are not in fellowship with Him, seeking Him, you are not "saved"—you are lost. If you say the "Sinner's Prayer" and "confess with your mouth that Jesus is your Savior" yet make no attempt to change the course of your life, be aware that the Bible is very specific about this as well.

I Corinthians 6:9–11 clearly states, "Do you not know that the unrighteous will not inherit the kingdom of God? Do not be deceived; neither fornicators, nor idolaters, nor adulterers, nor effeminate, nor homosexuals, nor thieves, nor the covetous, nor drunkards, nor revilers, nor swindlers, will inherit the kingdom of God. Such were some of you; but you were washed, but you were sanctified, but you were justified in the Name of the Lord Jesus Christ and in the Spirit of our God."

Some make light of the situation, of the need for a relationship with God.

"The Lord and I, we get along fine. We have 'an understanding.' I don't bother Him, and He doesn't bother me." I used to say this very thing myself.

It is a joke. This is done flippantly, with a feeling of daring; nothing happens, and eventually the heart becomes calloused, hard. For many others, they are afraid to show their love of God—and heaven forbid—their true passion. Those who believe in aliens, ghosts and horoscopes are much more vocal about their beliefs than the children of God. Music fans, racing and sports fans are far more devoted and avid than Christians, shouting and waving their arms. To shout and clap, dance and wave your arms in church is considered weird. Are you guilty of such behavior in church? I am. When Christ liberated my soul and spirit, He liberated my tongue, my hands and my feet too. When I worship, my entire being worships. I simply can't help myself.

But let us go on with this topic of different sorts of faith. Even an atheist has a type of faith, and that a remarkable faith indeed, for it must be very difficult to look at God's vast creation and steadfastly insist that all this exists by happenstance, by evolution from some chance matter. Even a "big bang" and that first molecule of matter must, after all, have a source and a Prime Mover, and that, we know, is GOD.

Psalm 14:1 says, "The fool says in his heart, 'There is no God ... '"

Despite all evidence to the contrary, those who don't want to face it will continually insist there is no God, or will ignore the fact, or will simply bear it out as irrelevant to his or her life.

"What difference does it make?" they ask. "God won't interfere with me."

Romans 1:20 says, "For since the creation of the world His invisible attributes, His eternal power and divine nature, have been clearly seen, being understood through what has been made, so that they are without excuse."

We cannot reject knowledge of God's power; we cannot deny His creative genius for we can see evidence of God everywhere.

It is said that there are fewer true atheists than proclaim themselves to be and more true agnostics (another sort of faith). Agnostics are those who are truly confused and don't know what to believe. In order to join the faith (yes, the *faith*) of atheism, one must truly be sure of one's belief in the existence of nothing. Most are instead simply unsure, simply do not know what to believe. Some are simply too lazy or apathetic to think it through. Agnosticism takes less faith than atheism and thus less work, for there is far less to meditate on, to study, to research, to question. One simply puts the whole subject out of one's mind. Agnosticism is less of faith and more of denial—denying the need to consider and think it all through.

There is also faith in oneself, the "New Age" faith in personal ability and achievement that takes so much stock in one's future. To that I say, what future? Look at our ruined planet, our clashing nations, our unholy and wicked peoples, and see whether you feel equal to conquering even your own small surroundings alone. I have seen several humanists that I am close to deny their need for God, affirm their self-sufficiency, and then come to personal ruin. One of them seems to continue to heap one disaster upon another and to have handed this life of calamity down to her children. She's been married to three abusive men, is constantly struggling financially, suffers ill health, and has freak accidents. Her grown children continually make bad decisions, also suffer financially and physically and are beginning to bear sick and malformed children. Yet after all this, rather than turn to God, she stands firm in her conviction that she is on a true path while following the teachings of a humanistic church and its pastor—not God and Christ. This is what secular humanism proposes to do; this is what humankind hopes to do without God. For myself, I don't even try to imagine myself without Him.

Now on a more personal note. Recently each of my grandchildren made a decision to follow Jesus. The discussions started with the usual question one would put to a child.

"Do you think you'll go to heaven when you die?"

The older two were sure they were "saved," and of these two, I was pretty sure my oldest grandson knew what this was all about because I had been talking about Jesus with him since he was a tiny tot. However, when I asked him how he knew he was saved his answer was rather startling. He told me he'd been saved seventeen times! This is the sort of faith that many have—faith for a time, and then it goes away, for it is linked to something temporary. Brandon had a temporary sort of faith that lasted from one "salvation" event to another and then he felt it was time to renew what he had done before. It's not that renewal is a bad thing—it is in fact a very good thing. It's just that once you begin a true relationship with Christ, you have it forever—if you care to keep it.

"I'm saved because the preacher told me I was," he said.

"No," I said. "The preacher cannot tell you whether or not you are saved." I told him that salvation is a gift offered to him exclusively from Jesus. The preacher cannot tell anyone whether or not he is saved. Jesus holds out a gift that he can take or walk away from. No one else can give it to him.

"You are a sinner," I told him. "I am a sinner," I said. "Everyone sins, no matter how hard we try to be good. We always do something wrong, we always mess up. But God is perfect. He never messes up. But He knew *we* would mess up, so He made a way for us to be forgiven. All we have to do is ask Jesus to forgive our sins, to take them away. We have to really mean it, to really want that. And if we do, Jesus is there and ready for us."

Brandon prayed, and he meant it, and he became a child

of God that day. He was surprised to learn that he thought he knew something that he didn't. Maybe you've made the same mistake. It's pretty simple really. We are not to trust in man's remedies—religion and rules, but in Christ alone. (See *How to Become a Christian.*)

On to granddaughter Ashley. "The preacher told me," she said. Apparently she had been going to church, going to the altar, with Brandon. While it is wonderful to know that my grandchildren are there before God together and that Brandon is helping his sister learn, it is not so good to know that they are learning some inaccurate things. At least they are learning *something* about Jesus though—and I know that Christ would honor their salvation. It is only that they are striving needlessly when they could be living and growing in Christ joyfully.

So I set Ashley straight too. Young Hunter was the surprise. He came to me before I could even get to him. I didn't think he was ready but he wanted to know. Hunter always messes up and it turns out his young heart was the most fertile ground. He didn't need anyone to tell him he was a sinner. He just wanted the remedy and he grabbed it like he was drowning.

These kids now understand that it's a conscious choice for life, that they now have to make daily choices to do things that will please God. I had chances to sit quietly and talk to each of them. Brandon thinks he knows what it's all about—feeling secure that Jesus loves him. I hope his security doesn't become complacency or self-righteousness and get him into trouble. Ashley Rose is the most serious and had some very sharp questions; she's a thinker, and I hope she keeps on thinking of Jesus, always. Hunter was full of questions, and I hope he keeps on that way, because that is the best way to grow.

Now here's the hard part for the kids' Granny. These three go home away from me where I cannot see them, touch them, embrace them, hold them, and pray for them in person. I can't look into their eyes and tell them it's all right. I can't teach them day by day and protect them from the sinful world, tell them that the garbage they see around them in the world—the violence and sex they see everyday on TV is not normal, that the drugs and alcohol and gambling and screaming is not what God meant as a part of everyday, normal life. I can't demonstrate for them the peace that God would love for them to live in. I can't model normal Christian life for them because I am not there. I wish that I could be, but God has removed me from their daily lives. That is faith in itself, because it takes faith for me to stay here instead of moving there and becoming part of their lives, because I could probably engineer that.

However, I feel deeply within my spirit that God is saying, "No, my grace is sufficient. Let it be."

It takes faith on my part to stay here because I just want to run to them and fix everything. And so, in faith, it is my duty instead to pray for them and remind them to grow up in Jesus. I hope our example can be of some worth, although they seldom see us. The final truth of the matter is as Jesus said, "'If you hold to My teaching, you are my disciples. Then you will know the truth, and the truth will set you free'" (John 8:31, New International Version [NIV]).

That's the sort of faith I have that takes me through.

Access to God Through Faith

"Everything is possible to him who believes."
—*Mark 9:23*

Moses asked God to go with him and his people, the Jews, "'For how then can it be known that I have found favor in Your sight, I and Your people? Is it not by Your going with us, so that we, I and Your people, may be distinguished from all the [other] people who are upon the face of the earth?'" (Exodus 33:16)

"'If you are pleased with me,'" Moses said, "'let me know Your ways so that I may know You and continue to find favor in Your sight.' And the Lord replied, 'My Presence shall go with you, and I will give you rest'" (Exodus 33:12–14)

God's presence in our lives is what sets us apart, makes us unique and special—makes it *obvious* that we are different. Without God's apparent influence in our lives, what sets us apart? This is why we serve, this is why we strive to live holy lives, to be something other than what those who do not know God are. It is because of God's presence in our lives and our access to Him through faith that we are different, that we are set apart. Because we are different, God treats us differently than He does others. He hears our prayers and answers us. People see this and respond to it, whether they will acknowledge it or not. Then when their hour of need arises, and whether they profess to a belief in God or not, it is to us, the believers, who they come seeking comfort, seeking access to God.

Our faith is based on this very thing, that Christ died and rose again. If He had not risen, everything we believe would be in vain, for we would have no remedy for our sins. Jesus would be like every other teacher, like every other prophet—a good "master" who lived and taught us good things—then died. As Moses beseeched God to accompany him and his people, we count on Christ to accompany us and help us as we strive to be different and unique—for what else will distinguish us and our people from all the other people on the face of the earth?

Our faith is based on the fact that Jesus is the perfect Lamb, the one last sacrifice for all time, for everyone who will accept it. Before Jesus, only God's chosen people, the Jews, could count on God's mercy, His favor, and His salvation. God sent them the rain in due season, blessed their flocks and harvests. God gave over nations to them, caused people to dread them and flee before them, leaving their lands and kingdoms to them. He blessed their women with strong constitutions so that they would bear many, healthy children, blessed their households with abundance. God made Covenant with His chosen people and only with His chosen people. In return, His people kept the appointed festivals and feast days, sacrificed their best animals and first fruits of their harvests to Him, worshipped and adored Him. There were hard times when they turned away from Him and He punished them, but they eventually repented and came back, and He restored them, because they were His. They were set aside specifically for Him. They knew it and everyone else did too.

Sometimes God was on the verge of destroying these people of His completely because He was weary of their sins, but then one of His beloved chosen people would remind Him of the Covenant and remind Him that He had said that the Covenant was forever. How would it look if the Lord destroyed His own people (Exodus 32:9–14)? So God would relent and His people would once again be restored to Him.

Under special circumstances others could join this Covenant people, but it was difficult and not done lightly. One could marry into the nation of Israel. Or, if one had extraordinary faith, one might be adopted in, such as in the story of Rahab (Joshua 2; Job; Psalms; Isaiah; Matthew; Hebrews; James).

The Jews' God is a holy God, awesome in His glory, unsurpassed in His mercy and grace. He gave His chosen people, the Jews such abundance, the very best of everything—lands filled with every good thing to eat, success in everything they turned their hands to, robust health, wisdom, beauty. When they traveled 40 years in the desert, their clothing and sandals never wore out (Deuteronomy 29:5). In return, they had only to love Him, to trust and obey Him—and all this was theirs. Was this too much to ask? To deny their God this due reverence and homage, this faith, this trust, this love and obedience—was to lose everything.

But these Jews, they were a proud, "stiff-necked" people—stubborn, sinful. God knew this. Was He then to destroy them? No. He knew them, for, after all, He had created them. So He made a way, a remedy, a cure for all this sin. It started so long ago with the first man Adam, in the Garden of Eden with the forbidden fruit.

"Adam," God asked, "what did you do?"

"It was the woman you gave me," Adam told God. "She made me do it."

Already at the first, man wanted a scapegoat. Already he wanted to shift blame, to find a way out. Just as we now want to deny that we are sinners, so did Adam want to deny his responsibility for the first sin.

Before we start blaming Adam and Eve for messing things up for the whole human race, let's be realistic about the human condition. If they hadn't sinned it was inevitable that someone else soon would have. It was inevitable that sin should come, for we are all weak in our flesh. We want what we want—we are tempted, we fall into sin.

God's answer then, as now, was not to destroy the sinners but to punish the sin. That first sin was covered by the first-ever blood sacrifice when God butchered the first animal and covered Adam and Eve's nakedness with the skin of that animal. Life is like that: messy, bloody. Sometimes it hurts, sometimes it kills, and it stinks. Adam and Eve were then expelled from the Garden of Eden to make their way through the imperfect, sorrowful, difficult life, clinging to what remained of their shredded relationship with God. The Bible tells us very little about what that relationship was like after the Garden, but we don't read any more about conversations in the Garden between Adam and Eve and God, or about God walking and talking with man. At this time, not only was sin born, but the natural plagues and scourges we face every day today came about as well—the things such as weariness with hard work; thorns and weeds; mosquitoes and poisonous snakes; wild animals—for God cursed the earth too (Genesis 3:17–19). The happy chapter of the blissful life in the Garden of Eden is closed, finished. Utopia is no more. But this does not stop man from looking for it and hoping for it. There is only one way to regain it, to gain access to eternal life, through faith in the precious gift of Jesus' salvation: through acceptance of that gift of salvation. Even though God shut the way to that perfect place for us at that time, He had already made a way for us to return to Him, through Christ and His sacrifice. God knew, Jesus knew, before that first sin was ever committed, that there was going to be a need for a final solution to man's wickedness and lost condition. (See *How to Become a Christian.*)

We must understand and grasp that God was not alone before time began. Christ was with Him. Genesis 1:26 says, "Let Us make man in Our image . . ." At the beginning of time, Jesus sat at the Father's right hand participating in all the Father did. God predestined, appointed us to be with Him; He also predestined a way for us to return to the pure and perfect paradise that He had created for us to share with Him, where He had sent us forth from. That knowledge, the knowledge of that place, dwells deep within our souls and spirits, in the center of our innermost beings as an inborn knowledge implanted as a seed within, one that causes a longing that can only be answered by God and a return to Him. There is a chord that is struck within us by God alone, accessible if one only allows it to be. It is the seat of truth, a vacuum that is unsealed by only one opening, a lock opened by only one key, that key being Jesus Christ alone.

We must reach inside ourselves and understand through God's Spirit the infinite nature of the glorious gift God has given—that gift that is the same as the temple veil torn in two, the gift of free access to the holy of holies, without rite and ceremony, without priest and sacrifice, for the Lamb of

God, Christ, has been sacrificed once for all. Who can know the mind of Christ? The answer is that we can.

God says very plainly that He has specific plans for us, plans to prosper us and not harm us, plans for a good future. He says that we only have to call on Him, pray to Him and He will listen.

He is very specific: "'For I know the plans that I have for you,' declares the Lord, 'plans for welfare and not for calamity to give you a future and a hope'" (Jeremiah 29:11).

God is waiting for us; He has made us for fellowship with Him. That is our reason for being, that is why we were created. If you are trying to "find yourself," look no further. This is it; this is your fate, your destiny.

"'Call to Me and I will answer you, and I will tell you great and mighty things, which you do not know ... ' says the Lord" (Jeremiah 33:3).

The sacrifice of that animal in the Old Testament days was instituted to cover Adam and Eve's sin in the Garden of Eden. That was the precursor, the forerunner to the sacrifices that God later established as the way for His chosen people to make themselves acceptable to Him despite their constant sinful ways. God understands the nature of humankind—that we are weak and constantly fall into sin. He understands this intimately, for He is our Creator and created us with this very nature; it is the very nature of our free will that causes us to sin. Our free will gives us the freedom to choose. This very same free will also gives us the freedom to choose God; that is the very reason we have been created this way. It is God's answer to the rebellious Satan. For Satan has told God that no one would choose, of his own free will, to worship and serve God.

This Satan, instead of serving God as he was created to

do, boasted, "I will ascend to heaven ... I will make myself like the Most High. . . ." (Isaiah 14:12–16).

In obeying, and exulting our God we abase, demean, and deny the claims of our common enemy Satan. We are God's own answer to Satan when we freely choose to worship, adore, and serve our God.

So this sinning also, because of our free will and often despite our best efforts, requires something of us that we can't, on our own, deliver. Because of our wicked condition, what must God do with us? Must He destroy us? But no, He still loves us—cherishes us—with all His heart. For His chosen people, His Covenant people, He made a way. Long ago, God made a specific Covenant with Abraham and told him He'd make a great nation of him, with children who would be far more numerous than the grains of sand he could see— so numerous that he, Abraham, could never even dream of counting them. God appeared to Abraham accompanied by two angels (Genesis 17:22). Mighty things happened. When God told Abraham, an old man of 100 and his wife Sarah, an old woman of 90, that they'd finally be parents, they laughed—but ultimately believed it. It was their faith that saved the promise for them. Then Abraham prepared a special feast for this Stranger and His attendants (Genesis 18:1). After that, Abraham prepared an altar and a sacrifice and God sent fire from heaven that fell and devoured the sacrifice. What a sight that must have been!

Later, when the dream of a son had been realized by Abraham and Sarah, God asked Abraham to sacrifice this, his only son Isaac. Abraham held nothing back. He gathered the wood and prepared to go up the mountain with his son. Isaac asked his father where the sacrifice was, and Abraham answered only that God Himself would provide the sacrifice. They traveled together up the mountain and when they reached the place of sacrifice, Abraham set about preparing the altar, laying the wood, and still there was no sacrifice but Isaac. So he took up his only son and laid him on the altar.

Then, as Abraham prepared to offer his only son to our Father, finally—finally—the angel of the Lord called to him from heaven. God had indeed provided a sacrifice, a ram caught in a thicket by its horns (Genesis 22:1–18).

There are so many things that are remarkable about this story. First of all, what must Isaac have been thinking? "My own father is going to *kill* me?"

Terror. But then, when it was over—when the sacrifice had been provided, slain, and offered—what an example of faith Abraham was to the son who he'd waited for for a whole lifetime! The other notable thing was Abraham's willingness to give everything to God—his great faith. But how grieved he must have been! Despite the fact that he couldn't possibly have understood what was going on, still he was willing to do what God wanted because of the Covenant he had with God. This was not an ordinary relationship he had with God. Remember—he had seen great things already—he'd met with God face to face, seen fire come down from heaven and devour a sacrifice, fathered a son in his old age. The third thing is a prophetic foreshadowing of a sacrifice of an only son: something Father God was going to do for all of us through His own Son Jesus' death on the cross.

Because of this Covenant with God, Abraham knew he must make sure that Isaac kept the terms of the agreement intact, that he stay holy, that he stay with God, in order to maintain this access to Him. So Abraham sent his servant to find a wife for his son from among his own people (Genesis 24). Isaac married Rebekah and through this union came the twin sons Jacob and Esau, "and the children struggled together within her" (Genesis 25:22).

So Rebekah inquired of the LORD why this was happening to her and He told her, "Two nations are in your womb; and two peoples will be separated from your body; and one people shall be stronger than the other; and the older shall serve the younger" (Genesis 25:23).

These two nations, Jacob, from whom came Israel, the Jews, and Esau from whom came Edom, the Arabian people, do not live at peace even today. Little else is said about Isaac, and if you look at what comes next, little needs to be said.

When Jacob and Esau became adults they became estranged. The Hebrew name "Jacob" means "heel-catcher," "supplanter," or one who displaces, usurps, or unseats others. So was this Jacob. By means of deceit and with the aid of his mother, he stole the blessing of his brother Esau, the firstborn son. In those early days, the blessing of a father was not something to trifle with; it was a prophecy that conveyed the fortunes and blessing of God Himself for the life of the one that received it—for the rest of his life, for himself and even perhaps for his children and children's children. It could not be revoked. Jacob usurped the rightful inheritance of his twin brother, and brought bitter enmity between them. So Jacob fled, because he and his mother Rebekah were (rightly) afraid that Esau would, in his bitter anger, kill him. However, God meant this as a part of His divine plan, and Jacob eventually was renamed Israel by God. It was from Jacob whom all the twelve tribes of Israel came.

Joseph, the favorite son of his father Jacob-Israel, was sold into slavery to the Egyptians by his jealous brothers. Later, when famine fell upon the land and the Israelites were starving, Jacob-Israel sent his sons to Egypt to buy food. Joseph had been prospered by God (Genesis 45:5) and was there to answer the need. Later, when the Egyptian ruler, the Pharaoh who knew and honored Joseph, had died, the

Israelites who had sold themselves into slavery for food under Joseph's rule needed to be delivered from a harsher ruler. God answered the need and sent them a deliverer in the form of Moses. Moses was sent to take them out of the bondage into a land that God had prepared for them, just as Jesus has been sent to deliver us from the bondage of sin into the promise of new life while still here on earth, and throughout eternity in a glorious heaven with Him and our Father God. However, we live in a bondage that separates us from God and holds us back from gaining entrance to this promise, much the same as the Israelites had trouble getting out of Egypt. Pharaoh refused to let the Israelites go—he wanted to keep his slaves. Satan does not want to let us go—he wants us enslaved in hell with him, as well as living in bondage as slaves to sin on earth. Moses led the children of Israel forth out of bondage; Jesus leads us forth out of bondage. The children of Israel had to be willing to go—many were not for they were afraid of the unknown. We have to be willing to follow Jesus out of our bondage of sin—many are not willing. Are you? (See *How to Become a Christian.*)

Moses met with God on Mount Sinai and God told him what was required for the Covenant people of Israel. These laws are many and difficult to follow. In reading the laws of God in the book of Leviticus in the Old Testament, we find that God's laws are very stringent, very rigorous, very stern and strict—they are so numerous and so many! They begin with the Ten Commandments but then cover everything from what to eat and wear (God even told His people not to wear clothing made of two types of fibers woven together—imagine!) to how to treat a rash or a patch of mold on one's wall. But, even though the LORD is exacting, too holy for man, still He is beyond anything we can imagine in compassion. He knows our natures intimately, for He created us with the free will that makes us the way we are. It is this free will that makes us sin, but it is also this free will that drives our faith, that answers Satan, the original rebel of all time when he says, "Why should anyone bow to You, God?"

In answer, because of us, God can tell Satan, "All these, My own, bow only because they love Me!"

We were made to praise, worship and adore God, and we do this by freedom of choice. We choose freely to worship our God because we love Him. Or, equally by choice, we choose not to worship Him, choose not to fellowship with our God, even as Satan chose not to worship Him. Satan's choice earned him eternal separation from God. For now, he roams the earth seeking those he can pull down with him; in eternity he will live in the lake of fire—hell.

This same free choice causes us to sin, whether we choose it consciously or not. So God has, in His utmost compassion and mercy, set up a way to take away our sins, to make a way to pay for the sin that would destroy us all. The clearest illustration of this redemption is a fine or judgment in a court of law. For a crime, one must pay. If it is a parking ticket, there is a fine. If it is a murder, perhaps one must pay with a life for a life. In the human court of law, for the most part, the punishment is commensurate with, fits, the crime.

God's holiness is so great, so pure, so awesome, that any sin is too much to be tolerated. We must be spotless to enter His presence. He cannot tolerate any sin. But, none of us—no man, no woman—can approach His holiness. All of us have sinned, none of us is holy. We are all guilty of sin, no matter how hard we try to be holy—and all sin bears the death penalty. So God has put in place sacrifices beginning in the Garden of Eden because He wants us so much—

because He craves us, craves fellowship with us, the people He made for this purpose. Through His priests, God set up blood sacrifices, sacrifices of first fruits of all His people had, of their crops, their animals, their goods, just to cover their sins—*not* to wash them away. What those sacrifices of the Old Testament did was temporary; they had to be done over and over again in the form of daily, weekly, monthly, annual, and other periodic sacrifices and rituals.

But these sacrifices of blood and oil and wine and goods were instituted only for His own chosen people and the very few who were allowed to join them. What of us, those who weren't His chosen people? God promised things would change one day, that Messiah, Yeshua, the Deliverer would come and the troubles of His chosen people would finally end—and that even the gentiles would then be saved (Numbers 24:17–19). This Messiah would be the final answer, would be the reigning King Who would bring peace to His people Israel, to all the earth—and solve all the problems of unrest, war, sin—and with this, all these exacting laws and sacrifices would end.

Over and over God told His people to watch—Messiah would come. The angels, messengers of God, foretold Him (Luke 1:30–37; Luke 2:11). Prophets foretold this Messiah while speaking the Words of God (Numbers 24:17–19; Isaiah 9:6–7; Isaiah 50:6; Micah 5:2; Luke 2:26–35). God Himself foretold Him (Isaiah 49:6). Then there came a "voice proclaiming," John, saying he was the one chosen to tell them to get ready (Matthew 3:3; Mark 1:3; Luke 3:4), that Messiah was really coming. You'd think God's chosen people would be thrilled. But their expectations were different. They weren't looking for a carpenter's son, a simple villager, one of their own kind.

Isaiah 53:2 says, "He has no [stately] form or majesty

that we should look upon Him, nor appearance that we should be attracted to Him . . ." Whatever it was the Jews were looking for in a Messiah, it wasn't the person of Jesus.

So Jesus came in the form of a child, grew to be a man, lived among His own people and taught in the temple there. His own people rejected Him and He gently told His dejected, unhappy followers that this was to be expected; a prophet is not accepted in his own home (Matthew 13:57, Mark 6:4). So He left there and traveled elsewhere teaching, healing, loving—gaining a following wherever He went—yet still being rejected by so very many, especially by the main body of temple elders and Jewish leaders. And the rejection continues today, for the majority does not look for the simple salvation through faith that He offers.

Why was their Messiah unrecognized? He was just not the king they had been expecting. Jesus came to deliver them, but they wanted deliverance from the temporal, physical, oppressive Roman government that made their lives so trying to them. They were focused on freedom, but on a freedom then and there. God wanted to grant them freedom from the law and they *wanted* freedom from the law—but the *Roman* law. They did not, for all their supposed great wisdom, understand the wisdom of God and the freedom He wished for them.

But these leaders would not hear Him, would not heed the words that He spoke, even when He told them, "'You diligently study the Scriptures because you think by them you possess eternal life. These are the Scriptures that testify about Me, yet you refuse to come to Me to have life'" (John 5:39).

God had prepared for them a Lamb, the Messiah, the Lamb of God, one last Sacrifice for all time that would break the bondage of the law of sin and death that they had always lived under. This Messiah, this King, this Deliverer, this Lamb of God, was to be a final Sacrifice.

So this Messiah Jesus ministered among the people for only three and a half years and became instead a bane, a nuisance, an irritation to the Jewish elders, a thorn in their flesh. He disapproved of their self-righteous ways, their lack of compassion, their failure to love. The people began to listen to this Jesus, to question Him, to talk about Him, then to *follow Him*. This Jesus seemed to be full of trickery—there were healings, stories of demons fleeing, the dead rising—but they couldn't catch Him at anything. Nothing could be disproved; He proved blameless of wrongdoing. What could be done?

They sent out spies, offered rewards. Finally one man, one close to Jesus, one of His own disciples, agreed to hand Him over. So they sent the authorities for Him and had Him arrested, had Him tried and yet—nothing. Again He was found innocent. But people could be bought—they could be bribed, and the mob ruled. They called out to have Him executed by crucifixion, a bloody, cruel death, a death fit for a criminal. That would be the end of this nuisance. That would silence Him once and for all.

But surely you know all this, so why do I retell it? The one thing in particular I want to tell is what happened *exactly as Jesus died*. As Jesus bowed His head and died, there was a great storm with thunder and lightening, followed by an earthquake. But the most important event of all is this: "And behold, the veil of the temple was torn in two from top to bottom . . ." (Matthew 27:51).

To gentiles, this is the most important Scripture up to that point in the Word of God. At that time, entrance to the holy of holies in the temple was opened to all who would come to Jesus. We know that it was at this moment that

Jesus cried, "It is finished!" And this is precisely *what* was finished: the Old Testament is finished and nullified; the New Testament is signed by the hand and blood of Jesus Christ. No longer is the temple and the holy of holies off limits to anyone but the Levites, the priests chosen to minister before God as God strictly outlined in the Law. There is a new law, a New Covenant, a New Testament.

This is in direct fulfillment of Isaiah 49:6 which says, "'It is too small a thing that You should be My Servant to raise up the tribes of Jacob and to restore the preserved ones of Israel; *I will also make You a light of the nations so that My salvation may reach to the end of the earth.*'"

The way is now open to all who would come, to Jew and gentile alike, to everyone—to you, to me. So now we are all free to come, to love and serve God because, as His adopted, we have been added to His chosen people. We are His chosen also, even if we are not Jews, "for the temple curtain was torn in two" (Matthew 27:51).

Now all who wish to come have gained access to the holy of holies where God dwells, for we are adopted into this family of His through the sacrifice of Christ Who paid the price for us all. Messiah came not only for the Jews but for everyone who would receive Him and His gift of salvation. No longer is the LORD God only for the Israelites—the Jews—for now all who will come seeking God through Jesus are God's "chosen." God has made a way for us to be adopted, to become part of those "chosen." There is no better news in all the Word of God! This event is the true end of the Old Testament, the Old Covenant, and the beginning of the New Testament, the New Covenant, the one that covers everyone, including gentiles, including you, including me.

It is because so many Jews view the Bible and the New

Testament as "gentile religions" that they do not know the story of Jesus.

When Jesus walked the earth and faced the Jewish elders and leaders, and they challenged Him: " … tell us plainly if you are the Christ . . ." (John 10:24)

Jesus' response was, "I did tell you, but you do not believe me" (John 10:24–25).

Jesus also bluntly told them, "If I do not do the works of My Father, do not believe Me; but if I do them, though you do not believe Me, believe the works, so that you may know and understand that the Father is in Me, and I in the Father" (John 10:37–38).

Those Jews who can be persuaded today to read Messiah's story see the Jewishness of the entire event—the customs and ways of the people, the ethnicity and traditions and beliefs. Many who finally do read it begin a serious study and can then understand that Messiah has indeed come in the person of Jesus. It is important that we also note Matthew 27:62–66 which tells us the story of how paranoid the chief priests and Jewish elders were that Jesus' followers might come and take His body and say He had risen when He hadn't. These things of the resurrection on which we base our faith for salvation we first receive by faith, but it is wonderful to know the history of that day as well—that there were soldiers posted there to guard the tomb. Matthew 28 further tells us that when it was discovered that Jesus' body was gone despite the seal and the guard, "they gave the soldiers a large sum of money … to say 'His disciples came during the night and stole Him away while we were asleep'" (Matthew 28:12–13).

All of these things tell us about what most likely went on that day. There are four gospels written by four men close to Jesus. One was a physician; he knew the facts of crucifixion—that it was unto death. There were stories by people close to Jesus incorporated into these tellings. Jesus' family was among these, including His brothers who He had formerly said did not believe in Him. Did they now believe? In John 20:17, after Jesus had risen, He instructed Mary to "go to My brothers and tell them I am returning to My Father . . ." Later we find them assembled with the disciples in Acts 1:14. What changed their minds about Him? The record is set down for us to understand how things were that day, but for the most part, we must accept what happened that day by faith.

Another note I'd like to interject is about the temple veil, or curtain. That it was torn in two spontaneously is not something to be taken lightly. This was a huge mass of specially, intricately woven material. The Bible describes it in the Old Testament as being 10 panels "28 cubits by 4 cubits" (Exodus 26). If a cubit is a measure roughly the length of a man's forearm or about 20 inches, my math tells me each panel was about 47 feet by 7 feet. If one panel was this large, the entire thing altogether was massive. One could not just take hold of it and rip it. This in itself was a mind-boggling event. The holy of holies, never before seen by anyone but the ministering priests, was laid bare before everyone. It was no longer secret; it was open for everyone to see. This most holy and sacred place was desecrated. Those Jewish elders and priests who could not accept Jesus as Messiah had this to contend with—the defilement of their holy and sacred place; it had been debased, violated. They had to purify it and reweave this monstrous covering.

By faith we accept that the sun will stay in the sky, that it is made of certain gases, that it will regulate our planet and make our food grow and warm us day by day and not fall on us. But we cannot be absolutely sure, can we? For this can end any day, just as our lives can. By faith we accept that the food on the grocery store shelf is safe to eat or that the water we drink is not killing us. By faith we accept that the schools will teach our children and not harm them, that history is more or less correct, that spring will follow winter each year. By faith we trust that our world will deliver continuity more or less as we expect it to. Every day is an exercise of faith whether we admit it or not.

We have faith in those around us to love us and trust us and in return, we love and trust them. Of course, there are breaches when people fail us, when we are betrayed, when things aren't as they seemed. People rob us, lie to us, betray us. But with God, there is a peace that never ceases, a peace that surpasses anything any man can give or guarantee. It is God Who holds the sun in place, holds us in place, holds us in His hand. His is the only one 100% guarantee. We all have some type of faith. God gives us sufficient evidence to extend that faith to Him.

When my walk with God is close, tight, right, I feel daily less troubled by the things of the world. For example, just now I think about my best friend Beth who has cancer. Frankly, it is hard to turn worry aside although worry is a strange word for a dedicated Christian. I worry that she will suffer too much pain, yet I know that because she belongs to God, God will help her to bear it. I know she will call me if things get too hard to bear, because she has promised me that. Then I know I will be able to pray with her and she will be able to bear the fear or the pain, because God has promised to be where two or more gather in prayer. (Matthew 18:19: " ... if two of you agree on earth about anything that they may ask, it shall be done for them by My Father Who is in heaven.") She is in God's hands, of this I am very sure.

But the flesh is hard to conquer. I wish I could whisk

her away to sunny Florida where I could seat her on the warm sands on the beach and pamper her, but frankly she's too ill to travel. I want to wrap her in luxury and make the pain go away and baby her. What I need to do instead is to give her back to God and let Him heal her—and to remind myself that even if she should succumb to her illnesses, that is healing too. What better healing is there than to walk in heaven with Jesus, in a pain-free, glorified body? It is we who are left behind who would be the ones suffering then, not Beth. She would be reunited with her other loved ones. I cry for myself without her, for the pain I will suffer, separated from her. Who can replace her? I beg God to heal her, and not take her away.

I think about this and I think about the others I've lost so recently and about how hard it is to keep losing people I love so much. We've lost George's sweet, innocent niece Faith, hardly more than a child, and our beloved, young friend Heather in less than a year. When I think about them, it still feels as though my guts are being wrenched out and the tears start again. I find myself rocking back and forth hugging myself, imagining it is Jesus hugging me. Each time I have to remind myself to breathe in and out, to wait on God while He helps me cope and the tears finally cease again—for now. I hurt so much. I've begged God to give me some space in time to get strong enough before I go through anything else again.

I thought for a while I was going to lose my Mom and I begged, "No, God, please, don't take Mom yet. I can't bear it!" Now I find I'm losing Beth too. Won't it ever stop—this life that hurts so much? But I hear the music playing in the background—"peace beyond the river . . ." Yes, peace for them, but what about me? But I can make it, because Jesus never leaves me alone.

I sit here and write and think about the world without Beth—how can I be strong without Beth? It hurts. It *hurts*. She knows me inside out. She knows what I'm thinking before I can even say it. She knows by my tone of voice when I need prayer even before I say so. Even as I write this, I know somewhere inside me is the ability to bear anything—*anything*—because God says He never gives us more than we can bear. I know this is so because I have this special access to Him—He is always with me. I can especially get to Him when it is most crucial. When I feel the whole world pressing down, I can throw myself into His arms, and He's waiting there—arms open wide. *That's* the type of privileged access we have—the type only His special friends had before—like Moses, like David, like Elijah. It's open to us now because of Jesus and that time on the cross, because He said, "It is finished!"

God is with us, always with us. I think of the poem "Footprints" by Margaret Fishback Powers, wherein a man dreams of his troubles and how he looked to God, feeling God had abandoned him, only to realize that God had carried him instead. I then reflect upon how God always carries us, how He is ever-present. There are so many places to find Him, but when we can't even look because we are too stricken to do so, He shows Himself. That is how much He loves us; He comes to us and picks us up and carries us in our hour of need. So I chide myself for my lack of faith when I find myself worrying about the things of life, because I really do have this ready access to God. He's always nearby. I repent of my worrying about Beth, about Mom, and turn things back over to Him again—and again and again and again. So instead, I pray and make up my mind to make my days count for more and give myself more to God. Life has no guarantees.

So we walk day by day through a life that hurts but that also gives us joy. The Word tells us that the upright will see God's face (Psalm 11:7). I so look forward to that day! I think about heaven most of all, about how, no matter how tough stuff gets, the endpoint is Jesus—blessed Jesus! Then no more sorrow, no more pain, no more tears or striving. And for now, there are so many times when I am so filled with the joy of knowing God's love and presence—it takes the sting out of the knowing that, like it or not, people are going to keep leaving us: Faith, Heather, my Dad, a beloved Auntie and Uncle, Beth, Mom, others. It's this access to God now that makes life on earth bearable. What would we do without Him? So let's make our best effort to dwell on what we have now, which is time to love one another and to love and please God, to live in joy and peace, because God has given us this ability through His grace and His Spirit. This fills me with so much faith for today and this deep abiding joy serves as a foretaste, a reminder of the greater joy to come—and strengthens my resolve to live my life in joy, doing my best to please God, to serve Him where I am, with what He has given me.

Because we have access to God through faith, our faith grows and we live by faith more and more. A life lived through faith is a life of growth. Everyday we grow more Christ-like, more God-like. Each day we learn greater ways to operate in the Spirit, for each day we find new ways to access the kingdom through the Spirit. We are awed by what God has for us on earth and this increases our faith. As our faith grows, we learn even greater things of God and so grows our spirit. Each day is a wonderful new journey in the LORD.

Sometimes, what we lack is simply an issue of circumstances. Sometimes my work seems like hard labor, some days the words flow smoothly and I feel myself exactly at the center of God's will. It takes more faith to sit and do the work when I am frustrated, exhausted and confused—so I get up and go away and come back later. Those are the times I know I need to seek someone who can pray for me and with me because my own faith isn't enough.

So, when things are too hard and you don't know what to do, remember that you really do have access to your God. Just believe and you will get what you've come for—sometimes it just takes time (I John 5:14–15). If you're stuck on something you've been believing God for, it's not that God isn't listening or won't answer you. God may be already answering and you're just not seeing the results yet. Or the answer may not be what you expect. He has made a way for you to the holy of holies through faith in Jesus and His sacrifice. As Jesus said, it *is* finished; the New Covenant is in place. Just keep praying and hang on. You really do have access to the throne room of grace.

Faith to Be Led

" ... not forsaking our own assembling together, as is the habit of some, but encouraging one another. ..."

—Hebrews 10:25

As we cast about for the solution to our lost condition we finally come to the answer, and that answer is Jesus. We accept His gracious offer of salvation as the free gift that it is. We are captivated, rapt, awed by His mercy, we are so gratified by His grace. Our sin burden is lifted and we are free. We love Jesus, we have a new appreciation for Who God is and we want to know Him more. The Holy Spirit draws us closer and we feel this tug, this drawing, this leading, and we want to follow it. We are, in fact, eager to do so, longing to know more of Him.

What then do we do with this saving knowledge? As new Christians, or perhaps as recommitted Christians, we look at a new Bible, a devotional guide, maybe a study course, and are zealous—for a while. We mean well, but life presses in, the books get mislaid, the language is perhaps a bit too formal—maybe even boring—and all our resolve simply seeps away, dissolves.

So we sigh and think, "What can I do?" We pray. We really meant our commitment. We *do* mean it. We want to go forward with Jesus, for we see that He is the best thing that can happen to a life, the best thing for everything that ails us and the wide world. We want to hang on. Our faith is real and Jesus is real. The Holy Spirit has done a work in us and we don't want to let go of that. The first steps have been so good and it has been so simple. This has been easy so far—for faith *can* be that simple. It is faith that has brought us this far, that has taken us back home to God our Father where we belong. But how do we hang on? How do we keep what we've found, know more of our God, learn to please Him and return His love?

While the next steps are not as easy as the simple faith that leads us to first believe, they are not so very difficult either. For now we "wait." We listen, we pray, we seek God's leading. Then *we go to church*. This step sounds so easy, so logical, but to some it seems to be something scary and foreign—maybe because it means negative things. If you are one of these, instead of putting this book down or flipping to a different chapter, let's face the problems frankly and work them through. Let's be honest about what the problems are and where they came from.

First of all, church is not an option. Church is meant to be the place of God's special presence. We must rid ourselves of the notion that "God is everywhere and in everything." This is a false notion fostered through misconceptions and misunderstandings. If God is in "everything" and is "everywhere" then He is in a strip joint, in hell and present in torture and in murder. He is in every abomination and in every dismal and horrific place. Therefore, this idea is obviously a lie from the enemy, false, and to be discarded. It is true that some of the translations of Psalm 139:8 say, "if I make my bed in hell, You are there . . ." This is a reference to a place of despair more than anything and indeed, if we go anywhere and have the Spirit of God within, He is with us there. This is a theological argument that we will discard in order to stay on topic. Another reference to God in hell is when Jesus Christ entered hell after His death on the cross to confront Satan and take the keys of death from Him; this was His victory for our sakes. The point of eternal damnation is separation from God in hell. God does not, otherwise, go to hell. Do not allow theological arguments about God being "omnipresent"—present everywhere—to confuse you.

The next thing about church is that people say it's "boring" or "doesn't apply" to their lives. First of all, church is about God, not us. We go to honor Him, not ourselves. Secondly, there are Christian churches today that speak to nearly every culture and taste from street art to high art, from cradle to senior, from hidden homeless to wealthy citizen, from physically challenged to physically fit. Having ministered in churches that make it their business to study the community closely in order to minister to "seekers" (those who don't particularly know God but are curious about spiritual things) for over fifteen years, I most certainly know whereof I speak. We studied trends in music, dress, entertainment, politics, society, education, even financial investment, in order to know what people were discussing and thinking. We did everything we could to bring Jesus, the Father, and the Holy Spirit to the people around us using the Word of God in ways that those we ministered to could understand through simple language in interesting ways. These lessons were enhanced through object lessons, professionally produced music, through drama and creative stage sets, through video production and mass media—all done by professionals and others with hearts full of love for God and a desire to serve Him and bring others to Him. Nothing was boring in the seventeen years we spent in that church.

As a matter of fact, many things were unexpected, such as the depth of the passion of our pastor, Dave Bowman and the many others with whom we served through the years. We will always thank God for allowing us to be part of such a vibrant work. Naturally not everyone fit there, but it wasn't meant to be for "everyone," only for those who had the same tastes. For those who do fit, it is their home, and for George and I, it will always be a part of us. We have moved on, but when we visit, it is still like family to us there. It will always be like that when we visit—like going home, for there is so much of our lives written in that church family.

Every church, like every family, has its own personality. Some churches are very formal, some steeped in the traditions of hundreds of years. Some congregations have church seated on sofas and easy chairs, some around tables in a bistro-like atmosphere. Some congregations meet on Saturday evening in addition to or instead of Sunday, some have several meetings a week, some only a few a month. Wherever you find your home church, there *is* one for you. God has moved upon the hearts of like-minded individuals to make a place that suits you, so don't be afraid. Nervousness is okay—many of us face that. But have faith. Then pull out the telephone directory or go online and start looking.

God wants us to live within a church as a part of a big, loving family. Before we found New Horizon Church (NHC) in Durham, North Carolina, we had been in a number of churches because none really "fit." But we went anyway and met people we loved and ministered to and with in different places as we moved about and sought God's will and plan for us. Although those churches hadn't been the "exact fit" for us, we stayed with some of them for a while, and ministered and worshipped with them, until one by one, we felt called out of each congregation and moved on.

We found ourselves being led away by God, released—and we went without even knowing where we were going next. Then, we'd choose another church and visit, maybe stay a few weeks or months, then move again as we felt God would have us do. We moved around like that for a few years until we finally found New Horizon Church—because NHC had not yet been born. Scary? You bet. After having visited seven other churches, we finally found one small congregation, perhaps twenty people, who had been meeting together for a few months. When we listened to Pastor Dave and worshipped with those few people, George and I looked at each other and we looked at our son and we smiled at one another and nodded our heads. We knew we were finally home. We choose to be led by Dave Bowman, and he became our pastor that Sunday and remained our pastor for over seventeen years.

God will lead you in this way as well. Visit churches until you know where you fit. It can be that simple. When we moved away from North Carolina and our dear church, we were nervous about the prospect of finding a new church.

"What if ... ?" I began to think. "Oh, no! Please, Lord! Not seven more churches!"

We were fairly certain God was in the move, for when we considered that we might not move after all, it seemed wrong. When I thought about not moving, I felt, very literally, ill. I felt a cold hard lump in my stomach, as though something would be very wrong if we did not move. I was leaving the ministry in NHC and we knew God was doing a brand new thing in our lives. I was trading all the various ministries of all the many years for the ministry God had been laying on my heart all the long years: to wait quietly before God in prayer and then write out the words He laid on my heart. So we knew we must do this thing, make this move. We knew we must have faith that God would find us a church, for we must certainly move. We knew we must have faith again to be led, for God had never before led us astray and He most certainly would not do it this time.

So be calm and have faith to be led. God wants you to experience His magnificent presence. He will lead you to a place you may have never imagined where you can do just that. In the book of I Kings, God took Elijah to a mountaintop and told him He would show Himself. Elijah protested that he could not go, for everyone knew that no one could see God and live.

God reassured him saying, "I will protect you. I *want* you to see Me."

So God showed Himself to Elijah, but not in the way Elijah expected—not in a wild windstorm nor in fire, nor in anything grand and showy but in a still, quiet, secret place within Elijah himself (I Kings 19:12). In much the same way, God will make Himself known to you when you bow before Him in His presence in His special place that He has prepared for Himself to meet with His people.

Not all churches have buildings that are grand and wonderful. For many years, NHC met in hotel reception rooms, dusty buildings, and schools. Finally, just after we moved away from North Carolina, they realized their long-awaited dream of a building all their own. It was a bittersweet occasion for us, for we had labored with them toward this wonderful prize, this place for our God, but we did not get to move into it with them. But now we are with a new and fast-growing church in Bradenton, Florida, and they have just purchased forty acres for a new building. Perhaps in this, the third growing church that we are partnering with, we will finally move with a congregation when they realize the dream of moving into a new building dedicated to our

God. Every other time we've left before seeing the church realize their promise of a new building to call home. But even if we don't, it's okay because churches are not about buildings—they're about people.

As you look for your church, never let go of the theme of this book: simple faith. God will lead you. He knows what is best for you and for your family. If something does not feel right with one church, go to another. Don't listen to someone who says you must stay within a certain denomination. Denominations have been and are born over opinions and differences in doctrine and interpretations of the Word of God. Don't get bogged down in this. Focus on salvation in Jesus Christ and on serving God. Perhaps you will find something that suits you better elsewhere. God does not love one denomination over another. Go where God the Father, Jesus Christ the Son, and the Holy Spirit of God as the three united Persons of the Holy Trinity are taught, where salvation through Christ is taught. Go where communion, the sacrament of the body and blood of Christ are given. Go where the Word of God is taught in language that you can relate to, that is clear to you. Go where your children and youth are trained in the LORD. Go where your family can meet and grow with other families. Go where your marriage can be supported—even when you're having troubles, so you can be honest about it and get some help. Go where you feel at home, where you can enjoy music and drama. Go where you can be hugged and eat good food at gatherings, where you can go on picnics and to parties to celebrate things. Go where the people make you feel good. Go where you can dedicate your children and your lives, where you can be baptized. Go where people will laugh with you and cry with you. Go where you feel like you're going to find some friends who will care about you all the time for the rest of your lives. Go where you will feel comfortable opening your home to others, where you can celebrate every day of your lives together with people who love God and will encourage you, and where you can live and die in peace. *That* is what church *really* is. That's what Christ meant His body to be on earth.

Then, when you get there, you'll find that all the people there are reaching out and pulling all kinds of other people in so they can get the same kinds of treatment that you're looking for. Then you can bring all your friends with you. Because *that's* what church is *really* about.

You'll know you've found the church home you're after when you can sit down in church with no qualms, no reservations at all, and listen and learn from your pastor. You'll feel safe submitting to your pastor as unto God, as Jesus' true representative on earth.

The Word of God says clearly "Every person is to be in subjection to the governing authorities. For there is no authority except from God, and those which exist are established by God" (Romans 13:1).

Just as you submit to the laws of the land—the civil laws of the city, state, and federal governments, so does this extend to the governing body of your church. Every church must have a strong leadership and it is to this leadership that you must submit. Do not be afraid to take this step, for you are to do it in faith. If your faith is in God and His Word, this step, like salvation, studying the Word of God, and finding a church, will be easy. It is a trust issue, another issue of pure and simple faith.

Trust God to take you to the right place and you will be where you belong, and so you can trust these people whom God has set over you to lead you. Every good leader (pastor) will have checks and balances in place, just as a secular government does, just as corporations and businesses do (or *should*). The pastors in churches who have such structures have less chance of going astray. I use New Horizon Church (NHC) in Durham, North Carolina, as an example because we were with them for seventeen years and they are an excellent model. NHC has checks and balances in place, not only for the pastor but for other leaders as well. With this leadership model in place, Pastor Dave Bowman is able to not only teach but to lead the congregation by example.

One such model is relational, between men and women. Pastor Dave instructs the leadership first and then the congregation that men and women should hold members of the opposite sex in chaste, pure and innocent regard so that they will not fall into sin. We were taught, for example, not to touch one another in certain ways such as hugging. Whereas hugging may seem innocent enough, full body contact of this sort between a man and a woman has potential for great harm. We were also taught that there were certain ways that women can look at or touch a man (such as rubbing the arm) that seemed harmless enough but that can send wrong messages, particularly from women to men, as men are more visually and tactilely cued, and more easily stimulated than women. We were also advised that members of the opposite sex needed to be cautious about meeting alone together, even in public, especially for meals, as there is something special and intimate about eating together. This was especially tough for some leaders, as they were accustomed to having business meals with clients of the opposite sex, and it was hard to obey. It was also difficult for some of the leaders who had to have ministry meetings when some of the other team members didn't show up at the last minute as scheduled and we had much to do and there were only two people then present—two leaders, one male and one female. But we adjusted, for we wanted to obey our pastor and make a strong and proper example for the rest of our team members. Hopefully from there it would trickle down by example to the rest of the congregation. How could we be an example unless we followed the instructions and did as Dave taught us? We were blessed by it, though it was sometimes hard to do it all especially when we were trying to conduct the business of the LORD. We coped, we managed, for we were submitted to Dave and we followed his lead and it was our duty to obey his teaching as leaders. By doing this we set an example for those who ministered with us, and taught them as well. This is what it means to have faith to be led.

When George and I moved to Bradenton, Florida we were nervous about finding a new church, for we were sure we'd never be able to replace our NHC family. After a few weeks when we had settled in, I started what I call the "church search." I called five churches and got no answer or no call back. Finally I called Bayside Community Church and the young lady who answered the phone had all the "right" answers. We wanted a church that emphasized intercessory prayer, community outreach, missions, contemporary messages that we felt applied for life today, worshipful music, and small groups that would help us stay in touch. Bayside seemed to be the type of church we were looking for. We visited one Sunday morning and loved it so much we went to "Bayside 101" that evening to learn more about the church. We loved *that* so much that we committed ourselves to the church right then and there. See? God was faithful and led us straight there. He knew our hearts were ready for a new home, and He was faithful despite our nervousness. He didn't make us go through the "seven church search" again. God knew exactly what we needed in a church and provided the perfect church home for us. We were ready to be submitted to a leadership under God; our hearts were ready to be committed. Now I have the time to pray and wait on God while He tells me what to write, just as I've always wanted. Simple faith. Perfect LORD. Praise be to His Name! We were nervous when we shouldn't have been. We had few misgivings about moving, for we knew that was right. But we were nervous nonetheless. We had left a church that was more than a church *per se;* it was family, closer than our own physical, blood families. They surrounded us when I was very sick and not expected to live. They were with us when we rejoiced, they cried with us when we were hurting. Our life was completely intertwined with New Horizon's. It was more than family to us; it was an entire life, a spiritual union, an association that cannot be explained outside of the entire experience of it.

To leave New Horizon meant to begin a life outside of theirs, to move away from family, to leave and go to a foreign place, to a place of strangers. But we felt we had a little safety net: a close friend and former co-leader in ministry had already moved to Florida. It is hard to tell how much it meant to have this friend in Florida. In fact, it was partially due to Kevin Hayes that we moved to Florida, for it was while on a visit to Kevin that we saw Florida for the first time. Prior to this, we had been feeling a growing complacency which began to alarm us, for we didn't want to be apathetic or "too comfortable" in our church. It was in coming to visit Kevin at the beginning of my sabbatical from ministry that our decision to move to Florida began to take root. When we moved, it was a comfort to know we had someone to relate to. In fact, when we moved and were very busy with the things related to the move, we went to church with Kevin for a few weeks before beginning the "scary" search for our own home church. Only Kevin was here in Florida, a small contact point like a lifeline, like the pin-point light of a laser beam. Deep down inside, we were unafraid of the move because we knew God would provide a new church home for us, and we looked at this as an adventure, excited to see what God would do. But we were a *little* nervous, remembering how long it had taken to find New Horizon. It sounds like a paradox, a contradiction, to say we were unafraid, that we had faith, yet to say that we were nervous. But God understands this. We were right though; we could never replace our NHC family. It was nice to have a family member here in Kevin though. Sadly, we seldom see him now as busy as we all are—but we have the promise of eternity together.

This, our life in New Horizon, and now with our Bayside family, is an example of what God has in store for each of us for our lives within a church body. He wants us to live within an "extended family" of believers. Once God leads one into a church, one must then submit by faith to the pastor and leadership, as the pastor and leadership have been placed there by God. I am not saying that pastors and leaders are infallible, for no one is capable of infallibility, of being perfect. Our very humanness causes each and every one of us to sin. Instead I am saying that when one is in a church, one is to submit to the authority of the pastor, and the leadership that the pastor has set up under himself. Everyone in a place of high leadership is called to be there ("No one takes this honor [high priest] upon himself; he must be called by God . . ." (Hebrews 5:4).)

Pastors bear an awesome responsibility. Their burden is heavy and constant. We, their congregations, as well as the lost, are always on their minds, in their hearts, in their spirits, even when they are resting, even when they are away. We follow them into their sleep, on their vacations. We are always with them. When we consider their leadership, we must consider our obedience as a duty to God. I do not mean that we are to follow blindly, for this is foolish and even dangerous. Instead I mean we are to submit prayerfully to a godly leadership as unto God in a body that is aligned with the Word of God.

I have heard too often, "I cannot relate to the pastor."

Pastors are not going to be someone all of us can fully relate to. That is because pastors are different, set apart for a special purpose. Pastors are cast in a different mold, so to speak, and are therefore someone we cannot relate to in the same way we do our other friends. I have noticed this difference in most of the churches that I have attended. Some pastors may seem preoccupied, sometimes aloof, perhaps even cool or unapproachable or distant. This should not be seen as a character flaw but instead recognized as a fact of their busy-ness and their need to handle many issues and people at once. They cannot therefore focus as fully as one might like with so many things happening at one time. Do not be offended with this supposed slight, for it means nothing. They are most often much more tenderhearted and attentive than you might suppose if you could only have them to yourself quietly for a while. God, knowing that these pastors cannot cultivate special friendships among this teeming mass of people, sends them associate pastors and other special close friends to work with and build relationships with.

Pastors always carry with them a special burden of responsibility on their hearts and in their spirits for the souls under them. How can we relate to that? There is so much going on in their minds, both consciously and subconsciously. They are very busy with the things of the kingdom, fulfilling the purpose for which they are set apart. I don't mean to say that pastors don't understand their people or aren't meant to be friendly to them, for they must follow Jesus' example of loving as we all must. Instead I mean that if we expect our pastors to be ever fellowshipping with us and knowing each of us personally we expect way too much. Even if we expect them to be attentive to our conversations on Sundays we expect too much. How many dozens of people can the pastor listen to when he hopes to be cordial and loving to everyone and not exclude anyone? How many close relationships can one individual expect to have? We need to think about what it is we expect of this one person.

The pastor of a church is not naturally more godly than we are and is as susceptible as everyone else to the same sins and weaknesses we are (Hebrews 5:2), which is why he is able to deal so effectively with us and our sins and short-comings, for he understands that humanness in us. This is why he so depends on our steadfast support; we must be unwavering in it. And it doesn't stop there. This love and prayer, support and fellowship must extend to the pastor's wife and children as well, for the leadership of the church affects the pastor's entire family. We love Pastor Dave and his wife, Sue, as family. We felt bound to them, responsible for them, for we labored together in the LORD. We felt that we must be sure to let them know that they were loved by us. We underwent the trials and growing pains of a new church together that at times tried us sorely. We opened our hearts and homes, we gave of our sometimes meager finances, we worked until we felt as though we couldn't lift one foot in front of another again, and sacrificed whatever we had to build a church where God said to build it. The church *was* built and stands as testimony to the fact that God is supreme and that we heard right, that we were doing what He told us to do. We suffered many things, but we did not suffer doubt, even though at times we wanted to quit because we thought the cost was too high, for we occasionally wondered how things might be if we weren't doing what we were doing. But don't think we didn't do it with joy, for with all the attendant trouble, the joy surpassed it all.

When Dave Bowman was led to Durham, North Carolina to begin NHC, he brought two close friends, associate pastors, to help him build and pastor the work. Over the last twenty years there were always others in the area and around the country that he continued to build and maintain relationships with—for he seemed to know instinctively that it was dangerous to be alone. So Dave sought other pastors and other godly men and met regularly with them for prayer breakfasts, for conferences, for retreats—even, I think, for recreation, just to be in touch with them. Dave has continually built godly relationships so he won't be on his own, so he will be accountable, so he'll have his checks and balances in place.

Then, if and when people would point fingers at him and say, "We think you're wrong here—we think you're off base and something's wrong in this church," he can always say, "I'll pray about it and examine myself to make sure I'm on course." Then he can call his prayer partners, these other fellows, and confide and seek God, and know for sure.

A few times there was an unrest, a rift within the congregation as people, overwhelmed by responsibilities and the cares of a growing congregation, squabbled and tried to wrest the leadership from Dave. Some were not even aware of what they were doing, I am sure. (They couldn't have been, right? I have to give them the benefit of the doubt. No Christian could have deliberately delivered such hurt to others.) There were politics involved, sin. For me, as a member of the congregation, a member of different ministry teams, sometimes a leader, and one submitted to Dave's leadership,

I suffered this with him and others close to him. I believed in what God was doing through that church and more specifically, through Dave. But it was more than that to me because I, personally, know how Dave is. I know him to be a man of faith, a man of prayer—and I know that he is on course and has these checks and balances in place. He can go to these others and say, "Pray for me, pray with me, because I need to know what's going on and I need to have prayer support—and I need it *now*."

Dave keeps his bases covered, so when the really hard times come he can be sure that everything is already in place. Because of that we could follow him in faith, submitting to him, knowing it was God's will. We could have the faith to be led by Dave, because we had faith that God led us into that congregation to be a part of the work of New Horizon. Dave's faith made our faith grow because Dave was demonstrating that he was being led by God. Part of this was demonstrated by his choice of associate pastors and co-leaders. With each step of faith Dave took, our ability to submit to him, and our faith, also grew. God gives us ample opportunity to exercise and strengthen our developing and growing faith by such things as this. God does not ask us to walk blindly. Then, we can, by our own faith, be the example that helps others to grow as well. Dave, as our leader and as a man of prayer, a man of God, would grow in closeness to God and we could see it; it was evident, as it was when Moses "went up to God" (Exodus 19:3). We could tell that things were right with New Horizon by the way things were conducted, by the successes that we had and by the fact that when things didn't seem so successful, changes were made. I don't want to make it sound like Dave is perfect or anything, because he's really a pretty "regular guy." Of course, *we're* apt to think he's great—because we love him and he's family to us. But he *is* a great example of a pastor, and a faithful man of God. He's even humble; he hates being in the spotlight. We just appreciated his leadership and his love—it's hard to say how much. He was just always there for us.

Through the years at New Horizon, Dave has had various co-pastors, associates, beside him at all times. Then, the day after Thanksgiving 2005, Dave and Sue Bowman's only child, beautiful Heather, died as a result of a tragic accident. There was such an outpouring of love from so many who had ministered with Dave and Sue down through the years, as former associates traveled from all over to be with the family. One then-current associate pastor, Bob Robbins, was beside Dave, at times constantly, much of the time with his arm around Dave's shoulders. It was good for me to see this, because when I think of Dave and know how sick his heart must be missing Heather, I think of Bob with his arm around Dave like that. I knew Dave was going to be okay because God had put Bob next to Dave for that very time. My faith for Dave's recovery was strengthened because I could see Jesus standing there in the form and shape of Bob, caring so very much for Dave, helping him make it through this, the toughest time of Dave's life so far. It eased my pain to see Dave and Sue enfolded in the arms of NHC and so loved. Heather is gone from me too—she was my child as well. As part of this New Horizon family, she was as a daughter to me; she called me her "other mother." So I am bereft too. Here at home for me, my family at Bayside Community enfolded and held me in their arms, and comforted me. I needed them to help me heal.

That's what church is supposed to mean and what having faith to be led by a pastor is supposed to mean. You start being led by faith and little by little it becomes so entwined with your life that it means everything to you. This is what "being in church" means. Being in church means belonging to a family of believers that becomes your whole life. Your church family will become dearer to you than your own flesh and blood, dearer than your formerly closest friends. They will understand how you feel when you hurt, how you feel when you rejoice, because they understand how being in love with God, how belonging to Jesus Christ, how being in tune with the Holy Spirit really feels.

So when you're "saved" and start wondering "what's next?"—*this* is what's next. Or if you are trying to build your faith, take a look at where you stand in your church. Maybe you're just a "Sunday morning Christian," just sitting back listening, just going through the motions. Maybe you don't know how to get involved, or think you don't have the time to do more, but there's always something. (See the chapter *Faith to Serve*.) Don't be afraid to be led into something more, for being involved in this place you have been led to by God is something really very wonderful.

When you walk in on Sunday morning and are truly where you belong, you can feel the sense of peace, the sense of belonging, the sense of excitement and wonder, even when things have been kind of hectic getting there and you're running a little late. Suddenly those things don't really matter—all that really matters is being there, seeing those shining faces. Even if you don't know very many people, they just seem very dear to you. You can bear all the fuss and mess that the week has been because you know that there are people there who really do understand what it's like. Even if they don't really know what you've been through, when they pat you on the shoulder and say, "Good to see you!" you know they really do mean it.

When I go to church, even when I'm by myself and I don't really see anyone around that I know (we're growing so quickly) I feel myself just grinning in anticipation of what's to come—looking forward to being in God's special presence.

So let God lead you to the next step, to church. Whether it's a church down the block or the one you went to when you were a child, or something brand new—*go.* Then when you find the right one, whether it's by process of elimination or by the "Aha! This is it!" method, you *will* find it. Just have faith. God will take you there. Pray. Ask God to guide you. He wants you to come to Him, to fellowship with like-minded believers, to sit at His feet and soak in His glory. It's so delightful, you can't even begin to comprehend it until you've experienced it. So go find it for yourself if you've not already done so.

Faith to Serve

"For even the Son of Man [Jesus] did not come to be served, but to serve, and to give His life as a ransom for many."
—Mark 10:45

When you've allowed God to lead you and you have, in faith, found the church meant for you, allow your pastor and leadership to lead you on a wonderful journey of serving God. When you find yourself in a position of serving, do so wholeheartedly, as Christ Himself did. Remember Christ's example of humility, how He girded Himself with a towel, knelt at the feet of His disciples—His co-laborers—and washed the filth off their feet. Jesus poured out His sweat, His tears and every last drop of His blood for us, bowed His head, and gave His whole life in serving us. That's His example, that's His kind of serving.

The apostle Paul wrote, "For though I am free from all men, I have made myself a slave to all, so that I may win more" (I Corinthians 9:19).

As a Christian in a body of believers, you will be called to serve in your church body. Every Christian is called to serve, no matter who they are or what abilities they may have, or what they may be able to do. Everyone has a role; everyone can serve in some capacity. There is rarely any exception to this, so be prepared to serve. Everyone can do something. Don't be frightened by this, for it is a simple matter. Some people think that they will be called to do something they will hate or will be unable to do, but this is not true.

Jesus says "My yoke is easy and My burden is light" (Matthew 11:30). This means that He never asks us to do things that are too hard for us to bear, for He bears them with us. There are many simple, everyday tasks that need to be fulfilled within a church that "someone" has to do. Just as there are many little housekeeping tasks needed to run a home, so is there much to do within a church. Anyone can pick up the stuff left behind after church, hold the doors open, or make phone calls for special events. Even when I was critically ill and bedridden for a number of years, I was able to do something. I was amazed at the number of times I was told that I had helped people so much with a word of encouragement, with a prayer, when I had no idea I was doing anything at all. So don't ever allow the enemy to say you have no gift or that you are too old or disabled or sick; everyone has *something* to offer. Have faith. God made you a unique individual, and He will show you what to do with your own special abilities in His body of believers. You may be surprised to find out how valuable the little you can do is considered to be by others.

Jesus tells us, "'If anyone wants to be first, he must be last, and the servant of all … '" (Mark 9:35) and, "' … whoever wishes to become great among you shall be your servant … '" (Mark 10:43).

True happiness is found by giving of yourself, by giving away your life. The Bible says, "Give, and it will be given to you. They will pour into your lap a good measure—pressed down, shaken together, and running over. For by your standard of measure it will be measured to you in return" (Luke 6:38). This is not only true in giving of your money or your goods, but in giving of your life as well. Until you can look beyond yourself, you will never see the needs of others.

General William Booth, the founder of the Salvation Army, was on his way to one of the first great organizational meetings of the group but was detained. When asked to make a statement that would best describe to the group the focus of the organization, he cabled one word: "Others." This became the focus of the Salvation Army and was indeed the entire heart and soul, the very spirit of Jesus' ministry. It must become the center of our own lives as well if we are to follow Jesus' example of ministry. You cannot serve inside your house, inside your head or inside your heart. You need to get out, to go out. In order to serve you need to go outside—outside your house, outside your heart, outside your self. You need to reach out. In fact, most churches have some type of ministries that they call "outreaches."

So begin in earnest to find some sort of service. Most churches today have some classes for newcomers that have a sort of survey of talents, experiences, likes and dislikes in order to get a feel for what people are able to do and so plug them in somewhere in the body. Most churches also have a number of small or home groups to choose from where one can meet and get to know people with similar tastes and backgrounds with whom one can experience growing in Christ. By joining such groups you will find opportunities to serve. Find your niche and find a place to get involved and serve. In doing so, you will find a fullness in your life that you have not known before, a true joy in living. Then as you serve, remember Jesus' example of serving—His readiness, gentleness, generosity and kindness, His love, compassion and ever-ready care. In serving you find yourself growing closer to God, just from the sheer joy of doing without expecting anything in return.

Yes, we are still human and sinful, but we become daily more godly because we are following in Jesus' footsteps, loving God, seeking Him, and serving others. The first commandment directs us to love God with our whole hearts, minds and souls. The second, Jesus says, is to love our neighbors as ourselves (Matthew 22:39). This, He says encompasses the whole law, for if we do these all else will follow. For how can we, if we love God and our fellow man, sin against them? In serving wholeheartedly we fulfill these two commandments.

In each of us God has placed unique and special talents. ("I will give thanks to You, for I am fearfully and wonderfully made; wonderful are Your works, and my soul knows it very well" (Psalm 139:14).) Each of us was created for a unique purpose upon the earth, and none of us were created without an opportunity to in some way serve or minister. We sometimes hear stories of the mentally or physically challenged or the indigent blessing others; how can we do less?

Let us use the analogy of a waiter or waitress. The waitress brings whatever is needed to the table to serve the needs there. Perhaps the table is completely barren—there is nothing on it at all. Perhaps there are not even any chairs there; perhaps the table itself needs to be put in place after the floor has been swept and mopped. The servers doing this are those who work on the very basics of church service, such as set-up, janitorial and things such as that; these are the people behind the scenes that no one is aware of—unless something goes wrong, something is amiss, or something is lacking. After being set in place, the table then requires basics such as napkins, silverware and condiments (the basics of the ministry, such as materials and goods). These things are provided by those who stock them and carry them in, take them out and put them away, keep them in order and make sure there are plenty of them on hand. When the people arrive, there are those servers who greet them and make sure they have "menus" (handouts) and a place to sit, who make sure they know where the restrooms are (which have been cleaned by those janitors), and where the drinking fountains are. Then there are those servers who prepare and serve the coffee, and provide special services (ushering with umbrellas in the rain, help with wheelchairs, directions to childcare). When everyone is settled by those servers, the servers chosen as leaders will minister in worship, prayer and teaching. During the church service, all participate in worship, which is our service to God. After the church service others will serve in the areas of prayer and counseling and other ministries as the people have need. At the end of all this, still other servers stay behind to clean up the coffee cups, napkins and remnants of the meal (donut crumbs, communion cups), sweep up, put up the chairs, pick up all those toys in the nursery, and generally close up shop.

But it does not stop here. The pastor, the head server, continues his service throughout the week. He carries the major burden for serving the people with him always, praying for and ministering to the people as they have need. He oversees his staff of servers as they, in turn, oversee their servers, and so on. This intertwined, interconnected assembly of believers serves one another and those around them as a pulsating, living, breathing organism, doing the work of the kingdom as an extension of all that is done within the church as it meets, and beyond the time it meets throughout the week in the lives of its people, as the natural extension of a living, breathing church. This is what God means for a church to be, a living organism, made of many people serving one another, and, together, serving others that need Him and need to meet and know Him.

So where do you fit in within all of this? Everyone can find something that suits not only their abilities and talents, but their schedules as well. If you cannot get to church to help set up on a Sunday morning, perhaps you can stay after and help pick up and put away. If you cannot work in the nursery because you can't stand to change dirty diapers or you're afraid babies might break if you touch them, maybe you can make phone calls or do some work on the church web page. Perhaps you can do some bookkeeping, or groundskeeping, or maybe you're a champion organizer. Whatever your abilities, you can fit in somewhere. The most important thing to note is that service to God is *not optional.* If you look down my "menu" of choices and can't think of anywhere you can fit, there is one area that fits all: prayer. Prayer is needed around the clock, any time, day or night. Every church needs pray-ers.

Jesus said, " If anyone comes to Me, and does not hate his own father and mother and wife and children and brothers and sisters, yes, and even his own life, he cannot be My disciple'" (Luke 14:26).

This seems stern when measured next to Jesus' usual gentle speech and attitude but it implies God's demand for our first allegiance when we come to Him. Serving God is not for wimps.

He takes us a step further when He adds, "'Whoever does not carry His own cross and come after Me cannot be My disciple'" (Luke 14:27).

I am not going to pretend that serving is always easy; I love to sit in my beautiful study and gaze down the street at the trees and enjoy the Florida breezes. It is often very difficult to stay on task and do the LORD's will, to sit and type out the words—make them filter from my spirit (I have to pray first), through my brain (I have to think about all this and study and prepare), to fingers and out (and then edit, rewrite, edit, rewrite, edit …). I'm not whining, for I love my work. I am instead saying that even the most beloved ministry to the LORD is not always easy. I hit a point when I absolutely cannot squeeze out one more word, cannot look at one more sentence and I'm absolutely done—and it's not even close to quitting time according to the clock.

I once served with a woman who wanted to start a ministry that she obviously sought as an "out" from a job she hated; she talked over half the time about how anxious she was to get out of that place. She could not—or would not—understand that to serve in a ministry often means to donate everything one can personally lay one's hands on, then to solicit others' help tirelessly as well. This usually means keeping one's job and starting the ministry as a sideline. I know what I'm talking about—I've been in that position often enough. To put it bluntly, you turn your pockets inside out and empty them, then beg for the rest. Yes, God does provide, but He expects you to do your part too. If you look at Luke 14 carefully, Jesus talks about a builder laying a foundation and counting the cost of the building, making sure he has enough to do the job. Then He talks about a king going into battle and numbering his army, making sure he can defeat the enemy.

Finally He says, "'So then, none of you can be My disciple who does not give up all his own possessions'" (Luke 14:33).

Now, of course, Jesus didn't mean that we all have to take a vow of poverty in order to serve Him, for if we did, who would run the government, the corporations, and the businesses necessary to the world, and who would support the missions and churches necessary to the work of God? Instead He meant to be ready to give all we have, to dedicate all we have to Him—to maintain a loose ownership of all we have, for it is all really His after all. For me, this has always been an easy thing—I'm not inclined to care much about my possessions and have few that I am truly attached to. My household goods are constantly in a state of flux—easy come, easy go. But some need to take this Scripture very seriously and to take a good look at how they feel about the things they own on this earth—and then to be ready and willing to let go of them. Or do we love our stuff more than our God?

To make a long story short, my friend finally managed to get the ministry up and running—after a fashion, but almost as soon as it took its first tottering steps it became obvious to all that she could not manage it. God will direct you to the ministry that He has chosen and equipped you for, to a ministry appropriate for you specifically, where He wants you to serve.

My parents were excellent examples of sharing and ministering to others in need; they showed us what it meant to give to others by their deeds rather than their words. I grew up serving others, sharing whatever I had with others, and it is a natural part of who I am. I believe that's the way God has made us, for it does bring a natural sort of joy. Seek opportunities to serve, no matter what abilities you may have, for there is so much joy in giving of yourself in this way. It is truly "more blessed to give than to receive," so reach out. The saddest people I have met in church are those who do not reach out and give, but who instead complain that they are "not being ministered to" or are "not being fed." If you feel there is something lacking in your life in Christ, examine your level of service. I do not mean to encourage you to serve to the exclusion of family life or rest, but to find something to involve yourself in that will bring you the satisfaction of belonging to and being a part of a vibrant, living ministry team.

When I was growing up, my family was very involved with our church. In addition to their jobs, my parents took responsibility for the maintenance of our church building. My dad worked part-time as the custodian, with us kids doing a few chores such as dusting, raking and other yard work, while my mom helped the aging housekeeper some, and older sister Sue helped with clerical and bookkeeping tasks. In addition, we were always present for the work that comes with the extracurricular and holiday festivities and fundraisers. We loved our church and were devoted to serving there. The priests were an extension of our family, the church our second home. This is the way church should be, and making it such can help families by keeping them closer to one another and to God. This is an added benefit of serving.

All of this service is—or should be—a natural outgrowth of our faith in God. It is as though our spirits are sponges soaking up the good things of God, then our services are those sponges releasing all those good things we've gained for the benefit of others. As we gain more of God our sponges are refreshed, washed clean, refilled, ready to wash over and refresh others. These sponges of our spirits are moist and plump, full of the fresh, clean, pure water of the Spirit, ready to provide again. Thus we can wash over those tired areas that need our service, refreshing, cleansing, renewing, bringing to the tables everything needed. Is food needed there? We can bring the nourishing food of the Word of God, readily available from the LORD, for we, ourselves, have just come from His table. Is simple hands-on service of another kind needed? Do we need to help someone with something? Since we are strong in the LORD (See the chapter *Recharging Your Faith.*) we can readily provide that. Is it counsel or direction that is needed? That too can be provided by the appropriate servers.

Whatever service is requested, we, as God's children, Christ's disciples, are ready to provide the service needed. We can answer the need, for we are ready as a well-rounded body of Christ, each member doing his or her part according to his or her unique, special talent or ability. We have come in faith, we have found Christ by faith, we have been led by faith, we serve by faith. Thus we are ready, by faith, to answer the needs.

Faith to Witness

"Here I am. Send me."

—*Isaiah 6:8*

Even though when we are saved, we come out of the world and become separate from it, there is still this walk on the edge of the world of sin that we must always continue so that we might reach into the darkness and snatch the lost from the enemy (Jude 1:22–23). If someone is lost to God, I must go where he is in order to bring him out. I may be afraid, but yet I go, for I am set aside to do this, I am taken out of the world and made to do God's work, anointed for such a time as this ("You have an anointing from the Holy One . . ." (I John 2:20)). This may mean contact with, friendship with, all sorts of people. The directive in the Bible is to avoid sin, not those who are sinful, for we are, after all, all of us sinful.

We know God's Word and strive to apply it daily, yet despite our best efforts we are still human, still unholy, still weak. Yet we try; we work at it. We also have to help those who do not yet know God's Word or who refuse to accept His directives for a holy life. What we must bring, demonstrate, is a knowledge that we carry in the heart, in the spirit, in the soul. If I have "hidden the Word in my heart" (Psalm 119:11) then I have the knowledge of what God wants and expects of me. Knowing my God intimately and being fully surrendered to Him, I am provided with the tools to overcome through the Holy Spirit. I must be willing and ready to answer when He calls on me and asks me to speak for Him. This is my directive, my duty, part of my service to God.

God calls us to holiness, even as He is holy (I Peter 1:13–16; 1:22; 3:9; II Peter 1:5). God expects us, through Him and His Spirit, to exercise self-control, wisdom and knowledge of what He desires in order to avoid sin and to live holy lives. As we strive to achieve this, our witness is our life, and it speaks volumes more than our words ever can. But we must always be prepared with our words—and the Word of God as well.

Jesus is the answer to everything. He takes us as we are. He takes us, disillusioned as we are with the things of man, with religions and sects and "isms" and tells us to drop it all and let Him have a chance, let Him explain the way He actually meant things to be. Because, you see, it's not about religion, it's about relationship. If I truly love as God wants me to, I have to give the best of what I've got.

Jesus in me says, "Let me show you a better way. Forget what the people in your past did, what some pastor did, what some church did, and listen to *me* if only for a minute."

This is what Jesus wants us to teach others. For me, this is a natural narrative flowing from my own history and experiences, both before I met Christ and since. This is "witnessing" as it should be. Our witness is simply our own stories of our lives and experiences with God.

I must always remind myself, "It's not how many words I say, when I say them, or how I get them out that counts, but only that I do it, and do it through Christ."

This is the assurance we have, that it's not our words we

utter, but God's, through His Spirit. Even if it's the "wrong" time or place, they will be fruitful, for His Words always have an impact and will never be in vain. I must simply have faith in what Christ can do with the pitiful few words I can speak in all my human weakness. Ultimately, the only way to truly care for those we love is to let them go, to commit them to God.

God says to us in Isaiah 55:11, "' … so will My Word be which goes forth from My mouth; it will not return to Me empty, without accomplishing what I desire, and without succeeding [in the matter] for which I sent it.'"

I keep always in mind what Paul the apostle said of the seeds of the Word of God: some sow, some water, but God gives the increase (I Corinthians 3:7). Somewhere, down the road, I just have to believe that these seeds I continue to scatter will take root and sprout. I keep in mind that what I speak may be the last time someone has the opportunity to hear the precious Word of God; it may be someone's last moment of life on earth. It could be the last breath that someone takes and God may take them and say, "What about what my witness said to you about Me? Are you ready for Me now?"

Suppose then, after a life of rejecting God, they finally say yes? But suppose instead that you or I hadn't said something to that person—suppose I hadn't said that one last thing—that no one had?

That's the moment we must have faith for. That's the moment for which we witness. We are not responsible for the response of that person, but for what comes out of our own mouths.

The Word says, "Now he who plants and he who waters are one; but each will receive his own reward according to his own labor. For we are God's fellow workers; you are God's field, God's building. According to the grace of God which was given to me, like a wise master builder I laid a foundation, and another is building on it. But each man must be careful how he builds on it. For no man can lay a foundation other than the one which is laid, which is Jesus Christ" (I Corinthians 3:8–11).

God doesn't expect the impossible of us—the saving of souls; instead He only wants us to do what He has assigned to us at a given time. The outcome lies in His hands.

I think back to September 11, 2001, the day the Twin Towers were attacked in New York City, and I think of all the suicide bombers who are deceived and commit their lives for a fallacy, for a false promise. I was sick with grief for a couple weeks. I cried for days thinking of all the people that died without benefit of Christ's saving mercy—without knowing that morning that they had no more time. I think not only of the innocent ones that died at the hand of the terrorists, but of the terrorists that murdered them. It hit me so hard. Most people cannot know when their time will be up. I have read some of what it says in the holy books of these terrorists and their religions are so strange. It's hard to stick with reading their doctrines because everything is so twisted. They start out logically enough, but then the lies begin. Why can't the people who follow these religions see through these lies? Why will they go to such great lengths to believe such convoluted, complicated creeds and not accept the simple truth of God's love? Why will they base their religion on hatred and maliciousness, and not on pure love and holiness? The answer to this is that their hatred goes all the way back to a sin of unfaithfulness, of mistrust, back to one deed in the desert long ago. God promised Abraham heirs as plentiful as the grains of sand in the desert, so many they couldn't be counted. When he was old, Abraham listened to his wife Sarah instead of to God and bore a son through her maidservant instead of waiting for God's promise. Abraham's wife got tired of waiting for a family and took matters into her own hands. The enmity began there between two women, between two people, and has never ceased (Genesis 16:1–5). Although polygamy was common in those days, failing to wait for God's timing was wrong, and the ensuing jealousy and discord between Sarah and Hagar was inevitable, for Sarah's barrenness was a highly emotional issue in a culture where children, especially sons, were the highest prize of all.

My heart is so heavy whenever I think about this ongoing enmity between the Jews and the Arabs. It's not ever going to stop either. We are instructed by God to pray for the peace of Jerusalem (Psalm 122:6), but it seems it's never going to happen. Israel as a nation struggles to survive and even as she gains territory and repopulates that territory, modern Israeli leaders come in and cede her lands back to her enemies in the name of peace. How can Israel ever survive like this? Muslim leaders are arrested and come before the courts cursing America and "praying" for her destruction, cursing Christians. They pray to the Muslim's "Allah," and we can follow this all the way back in the Bible to Abraham's misguided pact with Sarah's maidservant and his son Ishmael. Just as God promised, He made a great nation of Ishmael, but that nation has lived from the first in enmity with Israel and now with God's adopted chosen "Israelites," the Christians.

Too many believe that each "god" is equal (even the "god within" that is the god of so many millions lost in eastern religion, worship of nature, and humanism) yet the Bible says there is only One true God. The Word of God even says that millions will try to make their own gods equal with

Him. Why can't they see these lies for what they truly are? God Himself forewarns us that the lost will "exchange the truth for these lies" (Romans 1:25). It's all written there for anyone wise enough to read and receive, yet so many choose to read other texts and receive those words as truth instead, in the name of New Age religions, which are not "new" at all. So how can we teach the lost the truth of the proverb that there is "nothing new under the sun" (Ecclesiastes 1:9)? For some reason, there is the idea that these religions are benign, benevolent. They are far from it: they are instead volatile and intolerant in the extreme, teaching their people to war and destroy any who deviate from their beliefs and to murder the "infidels"—any who do not believe as they do. Why are we so deceived by all this? (See *Appendix III: Paganism in Our Homes.*)

At this writing there is a case involving a former Muslim who converted to Christianity who, upon returning to Afghanistan was found to be carrying a Bible and subsequently sentenced to death unless he would renounce Christ and Christianity. What could he do? At this writing, Abdul Rahman is still a marked man. If he is freed to leave the country instead of being executed as an enemy of Islam, he is in danger of assassination by his zealous, though lost, countrymen. But that is the price he pays for being a Christian, and he remains steadfast, even unto death. Would you remain steadfast? Can we do otherwise? To deny Christ is to lose eternal life—to lose everything.

Jesus told His followers, "'No one, after putting his hand to the plow and looking back, is fit for the kingdom of God'" (Luke 9:62).

In other words, if we can't be as steadfast as the Muslims are, we are not fit for the kingdom of heaven. If we can't hold out unto death as our brother in Christ, Abdul Rahman is doing, as the Islamic suicide terrorists do, we are not fit for the kingdom of heaven. (See *Appendix II: World News.*) We should not look at these as special cases but as part of the service due our God. Jesus served unto death; should we do less? Abdul Rahman is a witness as to how we should serve in faith. The world trembles and groans, shaking apart at the seams, and the people die daily in their sins, thinking they are going to paradise and reward because they have found a way they believe will take them to God. Then, in a hurry to fulfill their false path to this paradise, they murder and then kill themselves to get there. What true God would accept murder as a way to reward?

Jesus says "'I am the WAY the truth and the Life, no one comes to the Father but through Me'" (John 4:16). He proclaims it day by day through His living Word, the Bible.

As we pray for the peace of Israel, we become confused because there is no "peace." The Word of God says plainly that there will be no peaceful, united kingdom of Israel again until He (Yeshua, Messiah, *Jesus*) Who is appointed comes to rule. Thus, clearly, our prayer for the peace of Israel must be that they reconcile themselves to God and receive the truth that Messiah has already come, rather than a physical peace that they will never again see on this earth. Oh, that they would see this!

But God knows. He knew. He knew from the foundation of the world. In Deuteronomy 32:28 He said, "They are [a nation] without sense, there is no discernment in them. If only they were wise and would understand this and discern what their end would be!"

Recently a man I knew died. I mourn for his soul, for I fear it is lost. The only hope I have is that others close to him may have reached him at the last, for I know their hearts and spirits, that they love the LORD and have loving hearts. They told me that in the last years of his life he and his wife attended church regularly. But what I knew of his life told me there was no real change in the man he was. Those Christians close to him were very upset by his death, for they did not know this man's fate and whether he was lost for eternity in hell—for how can we know? We can only hope.

When the news reached me that he was on his deathbed, I mourned, because I thought I knew the condition of his soul. He cursed God continually during his lifetime. I tried to talk to him about the LORD once a few years back and his remark was as I expected it would be: "I've made it just fine this far without Him. Why would I need Him now?"

Actually his life told a far different story than his remarks did. His life wasn't "just fine." His marriage was obviously miserable. Daily he fought with his wife and she with him. It seemed as though they couldn't stand one another. He lived in a fantasy world where he constantly told stories about "girlfriends" that he had here and there, although it seemed that no one could stand his company. He used God's name freely as an expletive, an oath, a curse, with no more thought of what he was saying than as if it were any other word, damning this, cursing that. I once saw him backhand his young son for daring to make the sign of the cross with our Catholic family at grace before dinner. I don't know what ever happened to this man to cause him to be this bitter, but, from all appearances, he hated God.

I sat in the twilight and thought about all this, grieving. I felt that I did not actually mourn the loss of this man, for I would not miss his company. I thought that I did not love him, for I was not even fond of him. I suddenly realized that I mourned with God for a wasted life, for a soul who God cherished, for one who God loved as well as He loved anyone who He created. I suddenly realized that I *did* love this man, because God loved him. How must our Father feel if this man had died and slipped into hell, lost to Him for eternity? How did Jesus feel, after the agony He had suffered for the redemption of this soul, if He could not save him after all?

So I sat there and was surprised when I found that I felt like weeping after all. It was not for myself that I felt like weeping, but for my heavenly Father and for Jesus, because, in spite of all God does, it is not enough after all, for we are human and have a free will. Part of that free will is that we are free to go our own way and make our own choice, and part of that choice is to choose *not* to choose God, to choose to turn our backs on Him. The only hope is that those ardent Christians may have reached him, that something they had said—that their love of him—may have reached through his hardness and bitterness, and touched his heart somehow. Perhaps they had been able after all to persuade him towards Christ, and perhaps at that last moment, at that last second, when he saw God's face, he called out to Him for mercy.

That's why we must never give up hope. We must always intercede for the lost, pray for the lost. We never know when the hour will come for one to face God. We will never know when our words will stick by someone, whether they will find fertile ground or just lay there dormant (asleep), some day to take root. We never know when one word we speak will be added to the words of others and be built upon. We can only hope.

I remember my Grandpa was the much the same. Oh how he would curse! I remember my Grandma saying, "Merwin! The children!" trying to get him to stop his cursing.

He especially got wound up watching ball games. When he and my grandmother advanced in years, I wrote him a long letter and sent him a Bible, underlining and marking important passages.

In his latter years he lived in an apartment complex near my mother and father and often walked the few blocks over to their house. He came to their house one day and tossed my letter on the kitchen table saying to my mother, "That daughter of yours is crazy!"

I guess the strength of my conviction for Christ seemed too absurd for him.

My mother took the letter, folded it up, and put it in the drawer in the china cabinet in the dining room, where she kept other papers of his. In the letter I outlined the plan of salvation and told him that he had a responsibility for his spiritual condition and, since Grandma was sick, he was also responsible to see to it that Grandma's spiritual condition was okay too, since I couldn't get there right then and he perhaps could talk to her when no one else could. (See *How to Become a Christian.*)

The most interesting part of this story is that, whether he thought I was crazy or not, my Grandpa kept going over to the china cabinet drawer and taking the letter out and rereading it. Not openly, of course, but my mother told me she saw him doing it. The Bible I had sent him was among his things when he died, and was returned to me with evidence of having been read.

So be diligent. We don't know what people hear from us despite what they say to us or about us. We're not responsible for anyone's reaction to us. But we *are* responsible for our obedience to the directive to be ready to give the Word to anyone when the moment comes—when they may listen.

We go where we go day by day, and we must be sensitive to speak whenever we feel a prompting. We must be sensitive to the little urgings, these little proddings, for we never know when we may have a divine appointment to keep. If you find yourself in a situation where you feel you must speak, do it, for you are appointed to that time and place—you and perhaps no one else. If it burns within you, do not let the opportunity pass for you are responsible for that event and you must answer to God for your response to the moment. Do not remain silent.

Don't be afraid. They aren't your words you are speaking but God's. It doesn't take your power, but the power of the Holy Spirit, of simple faith in the power of God's Word.

"Who gave man his mouth? Now go. I will help you speak and will teach you what to say . . ."

(Exodus 4:11–12).

Faith to Live Out Your Life

"There is an appointed time for everything. And there is a time for every event under heaven . . ."
—*Ecclesiastes 3:1*

In the middle of the night as I sit up awake, I am struck as never before by something deep inside me. I have this keen awareness that one seems to have in the stillness of the night, and I contemplate my very existence. This is not all just some game—life—it is not some pointless seeking after worldly goods and fulfillment of passions. As there is a purpose for everything under heaven (Ecclesiastes 13:1), so too is there purpose in the Christ-driven life and those who are surrendered to God will find that purpose if they seek Him and His will.

The universal question of the origin of humankind, the earth, the very universe swirls through my overactive but tired mind. One may argue evolution, soupy primordial miasmas, the big bang. But the crux, the very heart of the matter is that first molecule. Where did it come from? Even to ponder happenstance or coincidence, one must have organized, intelligent thought to consider even that—to consider anything at all.

No, it's not a game. It's never been a game. This is a very serious thing, this decision to live for Christ, for to do so means that I may live persecuted (II Timothy 3:12), live outside the mainstream, live differently than many around me. George and I have entered a strange time period of our lives, a transitional time. Even as we surrender security in the natural realm, and even though we exult at the possibilities of what God may have in store for us for the rest of our lives, I know that faith in itself is not the answer. As I think about this move we have recently made to Florida, about what may yet be ahead, what we may do with the rest of our lives and why God called us here, all I can say with certainty is that we cannot be double-minded—we must be strong. Even over three years later I still think about our home and family in North Carolina and about the possibility of moving back there. But I know it's wrong. God has brought us here, of that I am certain. So I turn my back on those thoughts, turn them out of my mind and turn my thoughts back to what God has me doing now.

Even as I determine to serve God with all my might, to never compromise, to be the proverbial "shining light," still I think of what's ahead and wonder. I hope I can be strong for God; I hope that the fresh start will make me better than before. At times I feel as though my spirit pants desperately for God, as a deer in the forest running hard pants looking for a cool stream (Psalm 42:1). Then other times I am so distracted, so far from where I need to be, even lazy and doing nothing when I should be hard at work. Oh, that I may maintain my zeal and not weary! If I could only be someone who could constantly be surrendered to and only led by

God! If my worship life could only be as wildly surrendered as a kid dancing around or some fan cheering wildly at a ballgame—that's what God wants! Let me be as undignified in my praise as that—just like that and no less—only more! May I be humble, humble, *humble*—for who am I that God should even consider the likes of me?

> *"When I consider Your heavens, the work of Your fingers, the moon and the stars, which You have ordained; what is man that You take thought of him, and the son of man that You care for him?"*
> *(Psalm 8:3–4)*

So let me have a pure and undivided heart as I stand at the door of this new life that God has led us into. This door, the door of "what if" stands wide open, and we have only to cross a threshold to explore so many options. We can begin anew, take any one of so many directions. We have dared, as few do, to stop what we are doing and change course.

Upon entering adulthood such a situation is normal, usual. But to change course in midstream—middle age? To throw away the proverbial bird in hand to reach for the something else is weighed often by many, but the percentage of those daring to take that step of no return must be very, very low. So what have we done? We've looked around ourselves and questioned everything we have and have had, everything we desired and once sought. We've questioned our contentment and comfort and decided that we were too contented, too comfortable, so much so that we became lulled into a false sense of security. We were afraid that in such a false sense of peace we could become prey to the enemy, Satan, and so become complacent and no longer challenged to serve God fully. So we made this move. For what? For a chance. A chance at quietness and peace of mind in which to draw nearer to God, a chance to give more of ourselves while taking less from others in return. But is it truly a chance? Or is it the nudging of our Creator to follow His course with abandon, to take Him at His very word, to say, "We trust that You will go with us wherever we go in any circumstance, at any time, in any place or situation."

So what we have done instead of "daring" (for we don't feel very daring in doing something that we feel such ease and comfort in doing) is to take God at His word and allow Him to prove Himself to us again—and to others as He has to us, through our example. It gives us a chance to review to others our stories of faith in God down through our lives together in Him. For has He not saved us? Yes, oh, yes. Not only in our spirits and soulish creatures, but in our bodies, our minds, our very livelihood. He has healed us, led us down paths that are—though not always easy and certainly sometimes very difficult indeed—ultimately the best plans that He has for us.

We have traded striving in the ratrace to earn money that will fill our bellies with plenty enough food, for subsistence living. We lack nothing and are surrounded by comfort, by beauty, by the love of good friends. We are loved and love in return. We receive and give forth and receive again. Yet underneath it all there runs a current of dissatisfaction. This is all good; it is very good. It is good because we are challenged again and no longer complacent. We must think about the things of God, what it is He wants us to do. Something still tugs at us, ever present in the spirit, causing a soulish wistfulness not easily grasped. What is it? Oh, what is it that causes this petty little thorn? We are sometimes bothered by this thought in the back of our minds: is this what it's all about? Is this—excuse me for asking when things seem so good in America—*all there is?*

There it is. There really is something missing. Amid the

work-a-day week, the press of the crowd, the constant distraction of input from every direction, man stops to ponder. What the heck am I doing?

The answer is actually short and simple. We're living out our lives. We're doing what we were created to do … in a way.

The beloved and astute Pat Roberston once said, "Don't worry that what you're doing won't please God."

What? He explained that if we love God, have surrendered to Jesus with our whole hearts, and truly desire to and strive to serve God with our lives, then God is pleased. I've never forgotten that one small portion of his teaching. I love it. That means if I live in a slum or a palace, walk or drive a luxury vehicle, dig ditches or run the biggest empire of all time, I will serve God by loving Him and doing what I do, where I am, every day of my life.

Okay, so that seems simple enough. Right? Well, yes— and no. Yes, we can serve God where we are. But can we serve Him better by approaching this life thing in a different way? Maybe working some other job, living someplace else, loving someone more? That's what George and I are trying to discover—that's a big part of the reason we've moved. We were scared away from our old life by too much contentment, by a feeling of being lulled into a comfort zone and losing sight of all sense of challenge in living for God.

Jesus met a young man who was "good," trying to live a good life pleasing to God. Jesus counseled him to take it a step further by getting rid of his worldly wealth, for it weighed him down (Matthew 19:16–25). Our churches are full of good people living good lives. God is pleased by these people. But there's more. There's *got* to be more. Some try to find it in luxuries, but it is not there. I will not pretend to be wealthy, but having accumulated and discarded goods over many years, I can tell you satisfaction is not to be found in stuff. A thing of beauty, so said the poet Keats, is a joy forever, and while this may be so for a time, forever is a long while, and things do not last forever, so this is not the answer. King Solomon, the wise, pondered this as he did so many other things concluding that such things were as a chasing after the wind (Ecclesiastes 2:1–11). He knew that the answer was not in goods, riches, things, stuff.

Psalm 49:17 says, " … For when he [man] dies he will carry nothing away … his splendor will not descend with him . . ." So much for stuff.

What then do we do with this life? Why then do we labor day in and day out to scratch out a living, to keep up with the Joneses, to attain the American dream, to climb the corporate ladder, or, failing all that, to merely keep one's head above water and stay ahead of the game of life? Why do we go on working to fill our bellies and keep up with a house payment and car payment, and to keep the kids in clothes and shoes in the never-ending battle? God tells His people repeatedly that His fondest desire for them in setting up His covenant is that they live a blessed life, that they find satisfaction in all things. He wants us to be happy serving Him.

Our lives have a purpose and we (should) spend them in finding that purpose. The greatest, most obvious, and *happiest* purpose is to serve God. If we achieve this one objective, all else follows in due course, all else lines up, falls into place. Because one serves God, one can then claim all the Covenant promises of His chosen people.

Upon surrendering to Christ, our lives changed so rapidly it is impossible to credit anything or anyone else. I made my commitment to follow Christ on June 28th, 1977. George had made a commitment as a youth at camp at the age of fourteen, but had never lived it. After raising his hand in that camp service he escaped outside instead of going to an "altar call," so nothing ever followed his decision as a youth. But he remembered it and when I began my life in Christ in earnest, he too chose to follow Christ very soon after. We needed what all new Christians need: to be surrounded by people we could relate to so we could grow. The only Christians we knew then were my in-laws who were comparative strangers to me—and "not my type" at all (though very dear now!). Although I was sure of my commitment, I began almost at once to lose track of this new connection, to slide back into my old ways. I did not grow in God, for I did not learn from the Word. I had no way of moving forward. But *God* did not let go of *me*.

George and I had been living in Michigan for about a year and a half, and he was working with his dad and brothers. Suddenly, George and I both had the overwhelming desire to move back to Tucson, Arizona where we had just moved from. We put our house up for sale and, taking our few poor belongings in our old car, we headed south again. The only people we could find there from among our many past friends were two Christian women. One of them, Debi Amalong, had constantly witnessed to me, telling me about Jesus, while I, in my unsaved state, had laughed at her piety and cursed at her. That didn't stop her. All the time that we lived next door to her, she continued to come back to our house and visit me and to tell me each time that I was not happy, and that the only remedy to my unhappy state was Jesus. Debi's prayers were many and her witness bold and unwavering, and God now directed me back to her. Although we found an apartment across the street from three churches, Debi insisted upon driving across town many miles to come get us, then driving many more miles in another direction to take us to her church because she thought it was the most wonderful church in the world. At first I thought that was silly, but then I figured if it meant that much to her it must be something truly wonderful, and gave in. I pray that Debi finds this book, for otherwise I'll only be able to thank her in the kingdom for all she did to bring me to Jesus and teach me of His love and plan for my life!

The first time we entered the church I felt as though I had been hit with a wall of love. It was very real. I had never felt anything like that in all my life. People all around were singing and raising their hands, some people had tears running unchecked down their cheeks. I didn't understand what was going on, but I thought it was exquisite, very moving. We had to sit in the back because we were "late"; the service was going to start in 10 or 15 minutes. The place was huge and it was packed. This was the second service already. After that Sunday, George and I learned to be there early so we wouldn't miss anything—the music team came early to warm up and spontaneous worship broke out during this time. We never actually met many people within the church, but I felt as though we were a part of a huge family whenever we were there. It was in this place that we learned to praise and worship God with abandon. We were so excited we started going Sunday nights and Wednesday nights too. It was in this church that we also learned to tithe—to give 10% of everything we earned.

I fell so deeply in love with Christ that every spare minute was spent with Him. I immersed myself so deeply in the Word that I literally "lost sleep over it"—I stayed up late reading the Word and praying—yet I was never weary, never tired. I began to fast several days a week. George moved back to Michigan to work with his Dad and brothers again, but because I was in school and my tuition was paid, I had to stay behind and finish my schooling. My days consisted of getting our young son Kirk, then 7, and myself off to school, homework time for both of us after school, then some fun and family time, then when Kirk went to bed, the rest of the time was for the LORD. I spent hours every night immersed in the Word and prayer. We even took trips to the library so I could research the things of God. I simply couldn't get enough of Him. God showed me things left over in the house from when I was involved in witchcraft and I purged the house and burned the things I found, including things I had written. Without George there, I had nothing to distract me from this personal time spent with God and I grew in Him at a phenomenal rate. I can still remember the war I felt in my spirit, how I would awake at night and feel the presence of the enemy. I knew he was trying to regain control of my soul. But it was too late; Jesus had already won.

Besides learning praise and worship, we learned so much of the Word of God and His will for the lives of His people. My dear friend Debi made time for me any time I asked. When I was done with my classes, I would go to her house and she would teach me from the Bible. Her young son Jesse, age 4 or 5 at the time, was full of the Holy Spirit, and he would pray for me and tell me about Jesus. I learned to fast and pray. God revealed Himself to me through His Word. I was baptized in water and in His precious Holy Spirit. These are the fundamentals of everyday Christian living that God wants us to learn, that we may live under the wonderful blessings He promises His people. We learned there how to be a part of God's chosen, to know and believe His promises, and in faith to receive them.

God has so much for us. If you will sit down with the Word of God and read the Old Testament, so rich in God's promises to His people, you will find that He promises to give long life, health, prosperity, even honor to those who love and obey Him. George and I have never lacked anything.

My schooling was finally completed and George came back and got us and took us back to Michigan. It was okay now that I didn't "fit" with his family, for I could adapt anywhere that Jesus was, for He was all I needed and I carried Him within. We went back to the family church for a while, then found a church in our own neighborhood. Eventually we moved to a rural community in Michigan and joined a church there. Then when the recession hit in the early eighties, the family building business took us to North Carolina. Wherever we went, it was an adventure in serving God, ministering wherever He took us.

One summer several years later when we were living in North Carolina, our friends and former pastors from Michigan, Jim and LaRae Crawmer, asked us to come help them start a ministry in Indianapolis, Indiana. We did not know how we would make a living there or what awaited us there, and we were unable to sell our house in North Carolina, but we went trusting God that all would be well. So, we put the house up for sale, and trusting God, we left for Indiana in June. We helped Jim and LaRae start a small business there that would support all of us and the ministry. While George and our son Kirk, then 12 years old, helped Jim put out fliers advertising the business, LaRae and I stayed home and prayed for the business calls to come in. This whole thing was so exciting—LaRae and I would pray fervently, and the phone would ring. When we were not praying, the phone didn't ring. When we set about the praying again, the phone would go on ringing again. We quickly learned to spend as much time praying as we could!

During this same period in Indianapolis, many things

happened that were just too "coincidental" to *be* coincidence; they couldn't have been anything but God's provision. For example, having no furniture except waterbeds (they always folded down so nicely when we moved and we moved a lot), I said, "It would be nice if we had a couple single bed mattresses we could use like a couch. Then if we had company from out of town, they would have somewhere to sleep too."

When George, Jim, and Kirk came in from their flier distribution, they were offered a couple of twin mattresses, one like brand new, from someone who moved. A few days later, sitting on my nice mattresses, covered with a lovely quilt, I remarked, "I wish I had a chair over there so someone could sit facing the couch."

The very next evening, George was outside and a chair was sitting on the sidewalk. A man walked by and said, "Can you use that? The people downstairs moved and left it. It's a nice one."

So George brought me my blue velvet swivel rocker. Don't think that because we had secondhand stuff we lived shabbily. What God sent our way was always very nice. A few weeks later, another moving couple that we'd never laid eyes on before came upstairs knocking on our door and asked if we'd like three bags of groceries, because they didn't want to bother with them. Before that, I didn't know what I'd do that week for groceries. Another time we drove to church using the last of our gas with no money left, because we'd made a commitment to pick up an elderly lady, and she had no phone, so we couldn't call her and tell her we wouldn't be able to come.

When we got to church, the pastor came to us and said, "God told me you'd need gas money this week." He knew nothing about our finances—we were new to the church and didn't really talk about our finances to anyone—we "lived by faith." He pressed enough money into my hand to fill the gas tank for the week.

But I saved the best for last. The electric bill had come due and gone past due. I received a shut off notice and one other envelope in the same day's mail. The other envelope bore many red-stamped directions on it. It was a refund check from an insurance company that had followed us through three states and five addresses. I'd let you guess at the amount of the refund, but you probably wouldn't guess that it was the exact amount of the electric bill—plus a tenth above that, for we were (and are) still very much in the habit of giving 10% of everything we receive. This refund represented money from our "BC" days—before we knew Christ—and we wanted to give something of it.

Eventually we returned to our unsold home in North Carolina. I didn't want to go back; I wanted to stay in Indianapolis with my friend LaRae. I don't know if we would have had the faith to go to Indianapolis if we would have known it was to have been only for the summer.

Suppose God would have said, "Here's the deal. You're going to Indiana for the summer. I'm going to make the house payments in North Carolina, plus your rent and utility payments in Indianapolis, and I'm going to get you some furniture, gas money and groceries too. I want you to quit your job and sell your furniture and whatever else you have here so can to get the money to go to Indianapolis. Then you'll come back to North Carolina and I'll replace everything you need here. Okay?"

Would we have done it? Hard to tell. He's God after all, and He's mighty big. It's hard to say no to Him, but then we're talking about weak, ordinary people here. God has shown us so much of Himself, blessed us in extraordinary ways. Maybe if He asked us today we'd be willing, after all He's done for us down through the years. I hope we would—I like to think we would. We did, after all come to Florida in faith.

Faith for Eternity

"In My Father's house are many dwelling places; if it were not so, I would have told you; for I go to prepare a place for you ..."
—*John 14:2*

There's more to life than what I actually face each day. There's more to each day than what greets me in the morning, to what follows me into my sleep at night, to what drifts on my dreams as I slumber. There is more to my life than my hopes and dreams, more than my muses and wonders, more than what competes for my attention and allegiances. There is more to life than what meets the eye. There is more—there simply has to be more, for if there isn't more, then I give up. I refuse to live in this fog, this haze, this murky pall that is life on earth. Why do I refer to my life this way? The Word of God says that now we see the truth of what is as "in a mirror dimly, but then face to face ... now in part . . ." (I Corinthians 13:12). In eternity, we will see everything clearly, understand everything clearly.

So, I refuse to try and fail, to suffer day by day, to strive and scratch and only occasionally truly triumph. I simply refuse, for it just isn't worth it. But there is that which gets me up in the morning, that causes me to smile, that brings tears of tenderness to my eyes, that touches my heart so deeply, that strikes the one chord that tells me all this living and loving is worth it. That thing is the promise that my God has made to me, that He has prepared a place for me in eternity. He has a reward for me beyond this world. My God says that my striving has a purpose. He says that this path I struggle down has an end where streets are paved with gold, where there is an abundance in everything, where a place waits that I can not even begin to imagine. There the saints surround our Father's throne and praise Him forevermore. There we will rejoice together, laying down our burdens, living in the Light Who is Jesus Christ (Revelation 22:5).

There will be no sun or moon there, for Jesus the Lamb, the Light of the world will be the only light we will need (Revelation 7:16–18). The streets will be paved with gold so fine as to be transparent, as transparent as glass (Revelation 21:21).

There in eternity, we will rule and reign with Him. "And He will wipe away every tear from their eyes; and there will no longer be any death; there will no longer be any mourning, or crying, or pain; the first things have passed away" (Revelation 21:4); " … for the Lamb in the center of the throne will be their shepherd, and will guide them to springs of the water of life; and God will wipe every tear from their eyes" (Revelation 7:16–18).

In this kingdom God records our tears (Psalms 56:8)—each precious drop we have shed. All our sorrow ends there, and our Father has held each of our tears and counted them one by one. He alone knows the depth of our suffering here and wants us to know that He understands, so He has captured our suffering for all eternity.

Those who think that only those who have been nominated by the elect of God are "saints" are mistaken, for the Word teaches that those of us who receive Christ upon the earth and live for Him are saints. You and I, when we believe—we are the "saints." The New Testament is full of teaching addressed to the saints left here on earth, teaching on how the saints of God are to conduct ourselves. We have already been anointed and are being prepared for eternity. We will reign in eternity with God, and we are in training now. That is why it's important for us to be serious about our Christianity, about serving Jesus day by day wherever we are in the present. We must learn God's Word, and look at our lives as proving grounds, as a way of life not just for today but for eternity. God's Word is very clear on this subject, uncompromising in its clarity.

Many believe that eternity is nothing more than a peaceful non-existence, but the Bible teaches us differently. After death, those who belong to God enter "paradise," as evidenced by Jesus' statement to the thief on the cross next to Him on Calvary: "And He said to him, 'Truly I say to you, today you shall be with Me in Paradise'" (Luke 23:43). In the New Testament, the apostle Paul teaches us: " … we do not want you to be uninformed, brethren, about those who are asleep [dead], so that you will not grieve as do the rest who have no hope. For if we believe that Jesus Christ rose again, even so God will bring with Him those who have fallen asleep in Jesus" (I Thessalonians 4:13–14).

Then, after life on earth has ended for all, God will judge the earth and a millennial rule (1,000 years) will be ushered in on a new earth: "For behold, I create new heavens and a new earth … the former things will not be remembered or come to mind. But be glad and rejoice forever in what I create … there will no longer be heard … the voice of weeping and the sound of crying … no longer will there be in it an infant [who lives but a few days], or an old man who does not reach the age of one hundred and the one who does not reach the age of one hundred will be [thought] accursed.

They will not build and another inhabit, they will not plant and another eat … They will not labor in vain or bear [children] for calamity; for they are offspring of those blessed by the Lord, and their descendants with them. It will also come to pass that before they call, I will answer; and while they are still speaking, I will hear. The wolf and the lamb will graze together, and the lion will eat straw like the ox; and dust will be the serpent's food. They will do no evil or harm in all My holy mountain,' says the Lord" (Isaiah 65:17–25).

In the Old Testament, people were much closer to their God and more aware of the impact living for Him or without Him had on their lives. To turn their backs on Him had more immediate consequences. For example, to shun God meant to live outside of the community, to turn one's back on family and society. Today to avoid God and church is not only accepted but has little meaning—in most circles it has no meaning whatsoever. While it may grieve the hearts of some family members, there seem to be no consequences for those who do not go to church, do not worship or obey God. In the Old Testament when mankind lived close to God, to blaspheme, to break a commandment, to live outside the law may have meant to be stricken with a deadly illness or even to be struck dead on the spot. With the coming of the New Testament and the age of grace through the death and resurrection of Jesus, this old law passed away and we are free to live for or without God. Thus so many turn away without apparent earthly consequence and take no thought for eternity.

They do not even know what a statement such as the following means: "As for me, I know that my Redeemer lives, and at the last He will take His stand on the earth. Even after my skin is destroyed, yet from my flesh I shall see

God; Whom I myself shall behold, and Whom my eyes will see and not another . . ." (Job 19:25–27).

In the book of Job, Job told his friends—who for a while were his chief tormentors rather than his comforters (which friends should principally be)—that he knew that no matter what he suffered upon the earth, he would one day lay down in peace and wait for the day he'd be raised up to face God. Then, because he had struggled and remained faithful, he would see God face to face and ever live with Him.

In chapter 15, Job also says that man is born, endures for "a few days" (comparatively speaking when measured in eternity), that those days are decreed and limited beforehand by God, and that man "puts in his time."

He says that, unlike a tree that can sprout again, "So man lies down and does not rise. Until the heavens are no longer, he will not awake nor be aroused out of his sleep" (Job 14:12). We must be careful to understand that the Word tells us that man lives but once, then dies. There is no return of the soul for a second chance, no reincarnation.

This is why it is so important for us to read and study our Bibles. Some say they "read" their Bibles, yet only give it a glance or read a few verses from time to time. Some open their Bibles at random, some only use it in church. Then they read from the foreign teachings of eastern religions, and embrace these teachings rather than God's own, accepting them, rather than investigating what God's own Word says. Perhaps they read their horoscopes faithfully. Too many are beginning to embrace principles of foreign philosophies, which are really nothing more than pagan religions, and thus are led astray.

We need to be very serious about what God has to say to us. Only then can we be sure of what He has planned for us. These Bible teachings direct us that God not only has a plan of salvation, but is calling us back to Himself for eternity, preparing to receive us back to Himself (Psalm 49:15) to a very special place that He is preparing for us to share with Him for eternity.

How can so many miss this? It's because we don't know what the Word of God says, because we don't pursue the wisdom of the Bible. We unintentionally think of the precious Word of God as something stodgy, something boring, something we are forced to study, rather than the precious gift from our Father that it is. Then instead of poring over this glorious treasure, we dig into books and programs about philosophies tied to foreign religions and practices, never dreaming that the feng shui, the yoga, the meditations are based on the principles of foreign religions. We are interested in these "new" thoughts; we are mesmerized, and soon we are pursuing these principles instead of the principles that lead us back to God. I am not saying that all of these things must be taboo; Japanese gardens are lovely and yoga can be excellent exercise. Instead, when we seek peace and fulfillment we must begin with the LORD God, and always be aware which path we take, for our enemy Satan makes himself very attractive. If we do not always bear this in mind, he is able to trap us unawares. Let our meditations in our feng shui rooms and beautiful gardens be not pagan but Christian and let our thoughts be on *our* God only. (See *Appendix III: Paganism in Our Homes.*)

Why are we so easily led astray? Is it because we think the Bible doesn't apply for today? But it does! Is it because the Bible is perceived as boring? But it's not! It is an instruction manual as pertinent and relevant today as the most current Merck manual for your health. It has up-to-the-minute, up-to-date instructions for every facet of your life, for every aspect of your life. It addresses current issues such as family, social, political, economic, marital and other topics in such stunning detail that those who have never investigated it would be amazed.

If you think your Bible is boring, there are a number of reasons for this, the first being a lie perpetrated, committed by the enemy who does not want you to study God's Word and benefit from its power. The second most pertinent reason is that you are most likely reading a translation incompatible with your literary tastes or with your own understanding. I strongly recommend the New Living Translation for its clear, modern language. If English is not your first language, seek a Bible in your native language through the American Bible Society (1–800-Christian or www.americanbible.org). They provide Bibles in most of the languages of the world at very minimal cost so almost anyone can afford them. Almost all of the churches I have attended have given Bibles away to anyone and everyone, free for the asking. Another reason for failing to study God's Word is an inability to read well. Please pray and ask God to open His Word for you. You will then find that it is easy for you to understand, for it is simply written. Approach your study of His Word with the same zeal that you would approach anything else in your life that is of vital importance.

If you know someone who has trouble reading, please see that he or she gets tapes of the Word that are easy to listen to (not boring), perhaps set to music, even sung. There are contemporary worship tapes of Scripture verses that embed the Word simply by repetition through singing along with the delightful music. Go to your Bible book store and talk to the people who work there; they are a great resource. I use the One Year Bible as it provides a balanced daily reading. Each day provides a reading from the Old Testament, the New Testament, Psalms, and Proverbs. Thus you get the full scope of what God promises for living under His Covenant from the Old Testament (though we are under grace, not the law); the New Testament teachings about and directly from Jesus Christ and the things that apply to life in the Spirit; the inspiration of the Psalms; and the wisdom of the Proverbs.

As we grow through the Word and serve through our work on earth, we are being prepared for reigning in the new, millennial earth, and then for our eternal home in heaven. Those who are faithful with little here on earth will be trusted with little then, those who are faithful with much now will be trusted with much then (Luke 19:11–26). Our citizenship now is our proving ground for those ruling days later. Our true citizenship is in heaven where Christ is now preparing a place for us and is waiting to welcome us. That is our eternal destination. Until that time, we are to do our best here, preparing for what is to come (Philippians 3:20–21).

Has God entrusted you with many lives? Are you responsible to guide many, perhaps as a manager or teacher or as one responsible in the community? Perhaps you lead in the corporate world or are a counselor, doctor or other professional. These are great positions of trust and God expects much of you. The gifts He has given you are not to be taken lightly and you will answer to Him. You must be extremely careful in your walk with God, committing your life and work to Him so He may guide you in your work and use you in every way possible. This doesn't mean you'll suddenly be holy or supernaturally more fit to lead. On the contrary—you may find yourself stumbling more than usual, perhaps fighting feelings of pride. Or, you may feel resentful of co-leaders or co-workers who don't seem as serious or as committed to lead as you wish they would be, or as you consider yourself to be. The only remedy for this is to maintain as close a walk with the LORD as you can, being certain to continually commit your ministry work to Him, asking Him to help you maintain a pure and humble heart. It helps to always bear in mind that we are human and therefore so apt to sin, to fall because of our human pride. (See the chapter *Faith to Be Led.*)

If you pray for those around you and remain sensitive to God, He will make your work successful beyond anything you would ever dream. He will show you things you may never otherwise see about people with whom you work. As a lay counselor, I was amazed at the things God showed me about what was going on in people's lives and how it affected them. When I trusted God and spoke to them in faith about these things, it was as if a huge wall came tumbling down and all resistance to God vanished. This happened so often that there was no question in my mind that it was God Himself speaking to them through me, using me. It was not happenstance, it was not guessing, it was not luck or intuition. These were scary times for me, and these were humbling experiences. I did not want to tell these things to these people, because I didn't want, first of all, to be wrong, and I also didn't want to be telling people things I didn't feel it was my "place" to tell them. Yet God prodded and prodded and urged and pushed me until I did it, and I had no peace until I spoke and prayed with them. It became my "place" to say and do these things because God had put me in a position of authority over them because of the leadership position I was in. I was in that position because God set me there, under the authority of my pastor. I prayed about these things and consulted my pastor and between God and my pastor and with prayer, I obeyed and things came out right. In faith, I led others to a better place, a place more fit for these people to grow in God and toward eternity.

Prepare your heart daily in prayer to walk through your life with God. Open your day by committing everything to God. Even though you may not have a lot of time, make God your first priority. When I lived a very full life with many commitments (family, ministry, full-time job, mentoring, community service) our small group leader asked me to tell the group how I kept up.

I told the group, "I keep a color-coded calendar." I had it with me and I showed it. I kept appointments on my lunch and dinner hours. Then I said, "Actually the key is that every day starts with the Word and prayer. Period. Even if I have to be late for work to do it."

During that same period, I had a boss who said when I was late once, "So you're late. I don't even have to know why, because you must have a very good reason, and I don't have to know it to know that it's a good one. Never mind."

Hearing that made me feel good and reminded me that I was on the right path. I had actually stopped at a park along the way to pray because I had not had time at home.

I am not trying to tell you that this is easy, for it may be very, very difficult. You may become weary at times but, " … those who wait for the LORD will gain new strength; they will mount up with wings like eagles, they will run and not get tired, they will walk and not become weary . . ." (Isaiah 40:31)

You will find your strength always in the LORD. If you ask Him, He will never fail you. Never.

I remember during this same time that I was often exhausted, sometimes having to actually sit and wait until God very literally renewed me before I could move and complete a task. I remember as a children's minister starting a new program in New Horizon in North Carolina, then a young church, being beset with crippling migraines. I would drag myself up the church steps, mostly crawling, and begging the pastors for prayer before going to bring the teachers together for prayer, then going on to teach a class myself. I quite literally could not function, and my husband would sometimes have to nearly carry me. After the pastors came together and prayed for me, I would feel a surge of strength, get up, and go to minister. When I was done, I would feel, again, quite literally, spent. I would then go home and sleep the rest of the day.

You may think that this was too much and that I shouldn't have been doing all this and should probably have cut back my schedule, but all I can say is that I felt God wanted me to do these things. I loved doing them for the most part, but perhaps I really got caught up in busy-ness and took on more than I should have. There is a saying, "If you want something done, ask a busy person." I was one of those that rarely said "no." Eventually I did stop doing almost everything when I was crippled by an illness almost to death, but that is a whole different story, and you can see that I came through that too successfully, by faith. God is always there. Always. Just call on Him and He will answer. He is always faithful. Always. *Always.* I can't say that enough.

This plan of God's was formed before the foundation of the world and foretold throughout the Old Testament ("And all flesh will know that I, the LORD, am your Savior and your Redeemer, the Mighty One of Jacob" (Isaiah 49:26).)

Jesus' life, ministry, passion, death and resurrection wasn't a whim or a contingency plan. It was the way that was made for sinful humankind to find their way back to God, because we lack the holiness necessary to live with God. That is because rather than being perfect in holiness as God is, we are given a free will, one that gives us freedom to chose between good and evil. Because of this freedom to choose and because of our human, flawed character, we choose the wrong things, often habitually, forming defeatist patterns, caused by "besetting sins"—a continual commission of the same sins repeatedly.

The prophets down through time recognized their own sinful and lost conditions when they came face to face with God's condemnation of His creatures. Isaiah lamented his lost condition, realizing his inability to save himself.

"Woe to me!" he cried out (Isaiah 6:5), "for I am ruined! Because I am a man of unclean lips, and I live among a people of unclean lips; for my eyes have seen the King, the LORD of hosts."

Isaiah understood that, having seen God, he would die since no man can see God and live. We cannot bear God's holiness because of our unholiness, our sinfulness. But God made provision for Isaiah by sending an angel to purify him and make him acceptable. Then God showed Isaiah, as He had shown other elect prophets, His divine plan for all humankind.

> "... the LORD Himself will give you a sign: behold, a virgin will be with child and bear a son, and she will call His name Immanuel" (Isaiah 7:14).

After that, our Savior Jesus Christ came down to us in the flesh, and, as a man, walked the earth, fulfilled all the Scriptures written about Him, and died and rose again. Through His life, death, passion and resurrection He paid the full price for our ransom and bought us back so we could belong again to Him, to His Father. He ransomed us so we could take our place in the kingdom as joint heirs—not because we deserve it, because we never can, but because of His great love for us. That was God's great plan from eternity, that He should redeem us. Jesus has finished it, it is done. He has laid down His life for us and made us wholly acceptable to God.

All we must do is to find, to make a place in our hearts, souls, and lives to love Him. Can we do that? That's not much to ask for a place in eternal glory, is it?

Faith When You Don't Understand

"Blessed is the man who perseveres under trial, because when he has stood the test, he will receive the crown of life that God has promised to those who love Him."

—*James 1:12*

Jesus healed people then told them not to tell anyone (Matthew 8:4, Luke 5:14). Yet they did; they told everyone around them and spread Christ's fame. Why did He do that—tell them not to tell others what they had seen and heard of Him? Was it because He didn't want us to come expecting something from Him? Surely not, for we come expecting great things of Him, and He tells us to do that. Was it because He wanted us to come expecting only His love? Surely not that either, for He wants to give us so much more—He wants to give us newness—new life, a new spirit, a new start. Or was it because we are always contrary and do the opposite of what we are told? Perhaps it was that He desired that we not be distracted from what He is doing in each of us personally? Perhaps that was it—for He is a personal God, giving to each of us what we need the most.

We want to know God's mind, to understand and to trust Him, but some of the things that He does absolutely defy understanding. We are ready to receive good at His hands without question, often forgetting to return thanks or doing so only as an afterthought. We are perhaps all guilty of this at some time. We are filled with joy at prayers answered yet we do often forget to thank Him. Then there come the times of trouble, the times of disastrous difficulty and calamity when we wring our hands and weep copious tears and say, "Why, God?" We come looking to our spiritual leaders who can only shake their heads.

I am referring to the tragic times of disaster such as the tsunamis, hurricanes, wildfires, earthquakes, drought, flood, the terrible times of mass murder or genocide, terrorism and war, and man's inhumanity to man. Humankind seems to suffer more and more with each passing year. Many say that it is no worse now than ever before but that it just seems worse because there is so much more media coverage, but I disagree. I think it really *is* much worse, and I don't think this is a time for our Christian leaders to say to their people, "It's not anything we're doing wrong—it's not judgment."

It is instead a time to be honest, to stand firm and say, "God is making plain His expectations; He has blessed us when we obeyed and followed Him. So when we disobey, rebel and turn away, why should we expect Him to honor the Covenant we have abandoned?"

It's an unpopular stand, but it has to be taken. We can't continue to hide behind God's benevolence and grace claiming that in His mercy God would never destroy a city, wipe out crops, allow ancient, majestic forests to burn, and pests and diseases to devour crops, when clearly not only does He have the ability to stop such things, but He can and does. It is not so much that He calls these things forth (although

He most certainly can and will, according to His Word), but that through the natural order of things they happen, and He does not stop them.

With even a brief and passing, cursory study of His Word it becomes clear that not only will He not tolerate rebellion but that He will hold up the rebellious as an example to everyone else. "Many nations will pass by this city; and they will say to one another, 'Why has the Lord done thus to this great city?' Then they will answer, 'Because they forsook the covenant of the Lord their God and bowed down to other gods and served them'" (Jeremiah 22:8–9).

"Who is the wise man that may understand this? And [who is] he to whom the mouth of the LORD has spoken, that he may declare it? Why is the land ruined, laid waste like a desert, so that no one passes through? The LORD said, 'Because they have forsaken My law which I set before them, and have not obeyed My voice nor walked according to it, but have walked after the stubbornness of their heart and after the Baals, as their fathers taught them ... " (Jeremiah 9:12–14).

Further, God sometimes admonishes His prophets not to weep for—or even *pray for* such devastated peoples for His decision is made. "Do not pray for the well-being of this people. ... I will not listen to their cry ... I will not accept them . . ." (Jeremiah 14:11–12). His patience with them is at an end; the die, so to speak, is cast. He will tarry, wait, hold back no more, for His judgment is finally and ultimately come; warnings have ceased and the outcome is as He has decreed. Their wickedness has earned judgment just as He has warned, and indeed promised, if they would not turn back from their sin (Jeremiah 9:25–26).

There is a saying that goes: "If God does not judge America, He must apologize to Sodom and Gomorrah."

Do you understand this? America is the shining star of nations. We are held up before the world as the prime example of all that's noble and good, the so-called "Christian" nation. We are wealthy, privileged. Our poor are, for the most part, richer than some of the world's working classes. Many Americans, when asked what "religion" they are will say they are Christians even when they refuse to set foot in a church. In fact, according to a poll in May, 2006, 73% of Americans say they are "Christians." Yet corruption runs rampant in the American seats of power and we merely shrug as though we expect it. Daily, American financiers defraud the unwary of their nest-eggs. Parents torture and murder their children, children torture and murder their parents and peers. Every kind of debauchery is represented on American TV, on the Internet, and in the entertainment industry as not only harmless but normal, until we are so desensitized that nothing horrifies us any more. Indeed the entertainment industry uses horror as one of its mainstays, one of its premiere staples. It spoon feeds such things as murder, rape, drug use, robbery and gang activities to our children through the Internet, video games, comic books, cartoons, games, and music, and parents are for the most part unaware of what their children are involved in. The Internet is laden with so much readily available garbage at the touch of a button that extreme diligence and caution is needed just to keep it from inadvertently filtering into one's everyday e-mail. In fact, over-the-shoulder monitoring seems like the only way to protect our children. Or, if parents are aware, they don't want to get involved, fearing that if they object, they will alienate their children. And they don't want to do that, afraid to make "enemies" of their children. When parents are told to be aware of what their children are reading, too many say, "At least they *read*." They forget that their role is one of leadership and example, of guidance and direction, not to pal with their children. Children can find enough friends, but parents, supposedly, are limited. With today's splintered relationships, too many children may instead find a revolving door providing many parents with multiple partners who represent unstable parental roles that confuse this issue.

God even warns us that as we grow further and further from Him, even His prophets will fail. His "shepherds" (pastors) will spread lies. It is not so much that they mean to, but rather that they miss God, that they are not listening to Him.

This has happened to me, and it is frightening indeed. I was recently so preoccupied with "stuff" that I thought I heard God on an issue, but was wrong. Fortunately the issue was very insignificant (I can't even remember it myself now) and of no consequence to anyone other than me. I expressed it to no one other than my husband, but it devastated me that I missed God. I was so upset to think I had gotten so far from God and missed His voice that I weep even now to think of it. I repented and prayed and told God He could take everything from me—*everything*—my home, everything I owned, my husband, my life, everything, only please, please, *not* His Holy Spirit. It is that easy to miss God. I read my Bible, meditate and pray, sing and praise God, and attend church regularly, yet in all this, I am still missing God. How much easier is it for those overwhelmed with the busy-ness of life, who haven't the time or inclination that I do to focus on God?

Thus a pastor may hasten to tell his disaster-shocked congregation, "It's all right. God is here for us. He is taking care of us. He has never left us or turned away from us. He is ever-present."

All this, when in fact, God may have forsaken not only that city, but perhaps even that congregation in particular. We once attended a church that did everything it could to resist the new pastor in his work in the community, all the way to setting a meeting to have him removed for the simple reason that he dared to open the church's doors to everyone who had need of Christ.

I even heard people actually say, "Next he'll be bringing in alcoholics and hippies."

And thank God, he did. If you have ever read Frank Peretti's book *Piercing the Darkness,* it could have been written about this little church. But our Pastor Jim Crawmer and his wife LaRae stood firm and obeyed God before the onslaught of the enemy and the people that allowed themselves to be used by him. The sins were not so open as adultery and murder but were just as devastating. Everything that Jim tried to do they resisted. The backbiting, slander and rebellion were constant and calculated to undermine his authority at every turn. But Jim and LaRae stood firm until God helped us and rescued the church and turned it around. It was a miracle to see God bring these very same people to loving repentance in a meeting that was supposed to be a time to vote to have Jim ousted. But God's Spirit fell, and a time of healing followed. The congregation all gathered around him and poured out their love instead.

God had withdrawn from that congregation to an extent, but in time the people realized it, repented and returned to Him. Some very drastic things happened and it was clear that judgment had fallen on the congregation. But with God, all these things could be changed from darkness to light, and the church became a light to the community as it was meant to be.

" … among the prophets of Jerusalem I have seen a horrible thing: the committing of adultery and walking in false-hood; and they strengthen the hands of evildoers, so that no one has turned back from his wickedness. All of them have become to Me like Sodom, and her inhabitants like Gomor-rah. Therefore thus says the LORD of hosts concerning the prophets, 'Behold, I am going to feed them wormwood and make them drink poisonous water, for from the prophets of Jerusalem pollution has gone forth into all the land. Thus says the LORD of hosts, 'Do not listen to the words of the prophets who are prophesying to you. They are leading you into futility; they speak a vision of their own imagination, not from the mouth of the LORD. They keep saying to those who despise Me, 'The LORD has said, "You will have peace;"' and as for everyone who walks in the stubbornness of his own heart, they say, 'calamity will not come upon you.' But who has stood in the council of the LORD that he should see and hear His word? Who has given heed to His word and listened? "Behold, the storm of the Lord has gone forth in wrath, even a whirling tempest; it will swirl down on the head of the wicked. The anger of the Lkrd will not turn back until He has performed and carried out the purposes of His heart; in the last days you will clearly understand it" (Jeremiah 23:19–20).

As I have said, this is not a popular stand. We like to think of God as a calm, cuddly, Santa-like Grandpa, ready to take us on His knee and comfort us in our sorrows. He is love personified, but He is also *holiness* personified. If we refuse to accept this primary facet of His Person, we cannot approach Him through grace, for we receive His grace only through humility and repentance. Without acknowledging and asking forgiveness for our sins and receiving the gra-cious mercy and forgiveness only given through Jesus' sacri-fice, we simply cannot draw near to God. There is only one way to God, that being the repentant humility that takes us to Christ.

If you desire to have the assurance, the peace, of knowing that you are blameless in the midst of chaos and can run and hide your face in the shoulder of the Almighty, make sure you are innocent because of Christ. This is not to say that you are without sin, for none of us are. It means that sinful though you are, you walk in repentance. When you sin, you ask forgiveness, both from God and from those you may have sinned against. If you are not certain that Christ is your Redeemer, then take that step now.

If you haven't received that forgiveness through Christ yet, I implore you to do so immediately. Tomorrow is so uncertain. With today's catastrophes seemingly at a fever pitch, with wars and troubles surrounding us, how can anyone not crave the peace of God? There is only one way to the One true God. A simple prayer asking Him to forgive your sins and take control of your life is all that's needed. Then get to know Him through study of the Word, through fellowship in the Body of Christ, in a good, solid loving church. (See *How to Become a Christian.*)

So, when we don't understand—when our world is turned upside down and we cannot fathom what is happening, we can only hold on in faith. True faith says, "God has forgiven me and I am not guilty because Jesus paid the price for me. Whatever today and tomorrow hold, God will provide a way for me because I belong to Him and He takes care of His own—always."

That's His promise. Even in the midst of chaos, He never lets His own down. Despite what happens all around us, He will always bring us safely through. While we may never understand on earth why we may have gotten caught in the fallout of God's judgment, we must accept that God *will* judge mankind according to His Word. However, He loves not only those of us who have committed ourselves to Him, but each of us whom He has created. If we mourn for those who we love who are unsaved, think how much more our heavenly Father must mourn for all of those loved ones whom He has created. He so deeply desires to see each of us in eternity with Him. How deeply He must mourn their loss as they are swept into eternity, lost to Him forever! But, as we see in the Word, these times of chaos will come—they must *be*—and this seems to be happening with greater and greater frequency and intensity. Jesus Himself forewarned that in the end times there would be "'wars and rumors of wars'" and "'earthquakes in various places and famines'" (Mark 13:5–8).

Thus let us take it upon ourselves to more diligently pray and seek out those who do not yet know of the only way to God. In the time of trouble, let us, instead of questioning God, rise up with words of praise and comfort on our lips and let Jesus' Name be heard. Let us encourage one another not only with every material and physical comfort we can muster, but with spiritual, emotional, and psychological succor and relief as well. Let us be faithful to counsel tenderly, drawing people to God where they belong, keeping in mind that the history of man may well be drawing to a close. For how much longer can the earth shake and tremble, being poisoned and burned before it is totally ruined beyond repair?

> *"… but let him who has My Word speak My Word in truth"*
> *(Jeremiah 23:28).*

> *"'… Behold, I am against those who have prophesied false dreams,'" declares the LORD, 'and related them and led My people astray by their falsehoods and reckless boasting; yet I did*

> *not send them or command them, nor do they furnish this people the slightest benefit,' declares the LORD"*
>
> *(Jeremiah 23:32).*

While it is true that all of God's Word is to be taken in context, it is also true that prophecies in the Old Testament are given for the times in which they are spoken and are often for a later time as well. Notable are books such as Isaiah, Jeremiah, the Psalms and Proverbs rich in teaching relevant to today, as well as the Commandments handed down in Exodus. Many of the teachings in these books teach specifically of the Messiah, and Jesus quoted them often as the times unfolded, pointing directly to Him. Thus we must be careful not to say that these warnings about judgment that God makes pertain only to ancient times.

I am *not* suggesting that if someone is struggling with personal ruination in his or her life that God is judging that individual. These things happen to Christians and non-Christians alike. Do not look at someone having personal crises and think that this is happening because they have sin in their lives. Remember Jesus' admonition that "he who is without sin" is to cast the first stone (John 8:7), and that we are all sinners. Instead, come alongside such a person and offer all the help you can without thought that such a person is being punished. Consider Job, and consider also Solomon's ponderings in Proverbs. In these writings, the authors wonder why evil men gather wealth, prosper in health, live healthy and robust lives, enjoy their children and grandchildren, and die seemingly in peace. In reading the book of Job, Job's so-called friends persecuted him with musings about his sins that caused the supposed "judgments" that were his crises. We are instead shown what was really happening: Satan was given permission to torment Job in an attempt to turn him against God. Time after time, Job stood the test of his faith, and God finally rescued him, restoring him, rewarding him with an even greater abundance than before. While it is true that the good suffer with the evil in the midst of chaos, God does not single out individuals for punishment on earth. That He reserves for eternity, letting life play itself out here on earth.

The apostle Paul writes, "To keep me from becoming conceited … there was given me a thorn in my flesh, a messenger of Satan, to torment me. Three times I pleaded with the LORD to take it away from me. But He said to me, 'My grace is sufficient for you, for My power is made perfect in weakness.' Therefore I will boast all the more gladly about my weaknesses, so that Christ's power may rest on me" (II Corinthians 12:7–9).

I relate to this one particularly with the illnesses I suffer. I may well overwork myself and drive myself into the ground but for the limiting conditions I have. I simply must stop and rest or I cannot go on. I also must ask God regularly for the grace to sit and do my work, and must, in faith, get up and get to work, absolutely lacking the strength and physical energy to do it many days. This work I do is God's work and it is He Who is behind it. Without Him it could not be done; I do not have the physical stamina, the spirit or the power to do it myself. In fact it is a marvel to me the number of times I take up my Bible to search for a reference and to have it fall open to the very page where the reference is, and to have my eye fall to the very area where the Scripture is. How can that be anything but God doing the work for me and through me?

James writes, "Consider it pure joy whenever you face trials of many kinds, because you know that the testing of your faith develops perseverance. Perseverance must finish its work so that you may be mature and complete, not lacking anything. If any of you lacks wisdom, *he should ask of God,* Who gives generously to all without finding fault, and *it will be given to him. But when he asks, he must believe and not doubt,* because he who doubts is like a wave of the sea, blown and tossed by the wind. That one [man] should not think he will receive anything from the LORD; he is a double-minded man, unstable in all his ways" (James 1:2–7).

Then there is giving. I believe in the law of reciprocity, that if we give, God will give in return, in proportion to how we give. I am not talking about "prosperity" teaching as some believe, where we give to get. I am instead saying that if we give generously of what we have without thought of what we will get in return, believing that God will take care of our needs, He will indeed. He promises that. This is the one time in the Word when God says, "try Me" (Luke 6:38). God is faithful to bless us if we trust Him by giving back a portion of what He gives to us. I'm convinced of this one because we've done it since we've known God and we've seen Him do financial miracles all through our walk with Him. However I don't believe He necessarily punishes us individually for whatever we *fail* to do other than our own consequential loss of blessing for failing to do that thing and then reap the attendant blessing because of it.

In other words, God is *not* "out to get us." Instead, it is more a case of corporate culpability or fault, where many are guilty, through tolerance if nothing else: " … do not follow other gods to serve and worship them; *do not provoke Me to anger* with what your hands have made. *Then I will not harm you.* But you did not listen to Me … and you have provoked Me … and you have brought harm to yourselves." (See the *Appendix III: Paganism in Our Homes.*)

People have simply got to stop allowing satanism, paganism, witchcraft, idolatry and New Ageism to supplant

God in this nation. Otherwise, we are finished. Does that make what I'm trying to say clear enough? We were founded under God. If we don't stand for Him, He won't stand for us. Period. If this land is finished with God, He is finished with us. We can't just allow what is going on around us to continue, because we are just as guilty by doing nothing as we are by taking part.

America is far too guilty of calling itself a "Christian nation" then acting like a pagan nation in its disregard of God and His laws. Like it or not, the United States of American was founded on Christian principles, on the Ten Commandments, on freedom of religion, and on prayer. Our Declaration of Independence, our Constitution and even the money we so freely earn and spend reflect this glaringly. People may deny this and try to change this, but the proof is evident. I repeat: this is a nation founded upon God. If we don't conform to the standards that have caused God's blessing upon this nation, if we remain intent upon pulling down the precepts upon which this Christian nation was founded, if we are successful in setting up an atheistic, humanistic government in its place, God's mercy, grace and protection will be withdrawn and we will be on our own.

We are on a collision course with God's wrath because we are a culture saturated with media that can take us to God's Word at the touch of a button, yet we refuse it. Like stubborn children, we squeeze our eyes shut, and shake our heads, flatly refusing to have anything to do with it.

The Word says, "The evil deeds of a wicked man ensnare him; the cords of his sin hold him fast. He will die for lack of discipline, led astray by his own folly" (Proverbs 5:22–23).

That's simple enough. But instead we say, "God wouldn't do anything like this! God is too great, too gentle, too kind, to cause or allow this kind of devastation!"

But God is not the creator of this evil. Genesis 1:31 says, "God saw all that He had made, and behold, it was very good."

Instead, it is man's choice to follow his evil desires which in turn lead to evil actions. This sin life causes the woes of the world (James 1:14–15), not God. It was at the point of separation in the Garden of Eden when sin entered in that natural evil was also born and the earth was cursed along with mankind: "Cursed is the ground because of you; in toil you will eat of it all the days of your life. Both thorns and thistles it shall grow for you . . ." (Genesis 3:17–18).

Although God is not the author of evil (Satan is), He can use the sorrow in our lives to help us turn away from sin and seek eternal life. Thus we should try not to regret His sending it (I Corinthians 2:9) no matter how hard it is to bear, for we do not understand the things of God and what He has prepared for us, both in this life and the one to come.

People say that God would not bring devastation or destruction upon the world because He is too good and loving. They say that He would not allow suffering. Failing that, they question Him and say, "Why would a loving God do such a thing, allow such things as this?"

It is the failure of mankind, of our finite minds to think as God does that causes such questions, for indeed, who knows God's mind? Is it possible that most people don't have any clue what God would or wouldn't do in any situation? It is entirely possible that God *would* allow this type of devastation. God may very likely be *finished* with us, with our sinful, wicked, backslidden condition. He may very well continue to allow the chaotic conditions we've know the last few years unless humankind makes some drastic changes. Things may get steadily worse instead of better. This is a hard thing to say, and I do not say it lightly. Our God is a loving God, but He is also a *holy* God, and a covenant God. Covenants are legal contracts, agreements that are two-party involvements; they are "if-then" circumstances—if one party does something, the other party will do something in return. Too many people have the attitude of "rules are made to be broken," yet covenants are meant to be kept.

If you search the Scriptures, God says He begins His judgment with His own people, then He begins to list name after name of all the countries and peoples of the world and finally says, " … and all the kings of the north, near and far, one with another; and *all the kingdoms of the earth which are upon the face of the ground . . .*" (Jeremiah 25:26).

> " … *For behold, I am beginning to work calamity in [this] city which is called by My name, and shall you be completely free from punishment? You will not be free from punishment; for I am summoning a sword against all the inhabitants of the earth,' declares the* LORD *of hosts*"
>
> *(Jeremiah 25:29).*

God says He begins the judgment and cleansing among His own people. But, you say, that's in the Old Testament. Yes. But will He, in the age of grace, under the New Testament with our special freedom, hold us blameless? I cannot say. I like to think that because we have the Perfect Sacrifice (Jesus) that washes away instead of covering our sins that we are exempt from judgment on the earth, but God doesn't tell us that. Instead we are told by Jesus to live holy lives, to do well, to be godly. I am not saying that God will come down and strike us for our failures, but instead we won't receive all the blessings He has for us, including His awesome protection upon us all. We may be instead sitting in the fallout of disaster and ruin. I look at the countries whose principal religions are pagan and who persecute and exclude Christians and see the extent to which they suffer famine, natural disasters and wars. The deepening degree of their disasters lead me to contemplate whether God may not have withdrawn His mercy from them, and whether His judgment may not be falling upon them. Consider the Buddhist and Hindu nations where the people die on the sidewalks and trample one another at the shrines and on pilgrimages to their pagan gods. Is the One true God reigning supreme there? Are they living and dying without Him? Is it possible that He has left them alone? Our missionaries may well be working against the clock in those areas. We cannot know how much time we have left to bring in the souls of these worlds apart from the comfortable "Christian world" that we inhabit.

But again, this is not to say that even when we Christians are doing well things may not go wrong. Sometimes things happen that we absolutely, positively cannot understand, that don't seem tied to anything that is going on, to anything that has happened. Everything seems to be running smoothly. We are good with God, our walk with Him is solid. We are examining ourselves, living closely with the LORD, blessed in all things. Then, out of the blue—disaster! What has happened? Why has this occurred? What is going on?

I very recently lost a dear, sweet young friend, the only child of our former pastor and his wife, close friends, Dave and Sue Bowman. Heather and I were once very close; she was as close as a daughter. I think of her beautiful face, her vivacious spirit, the times we shared, the way she hugged me like she was clinging to me for dear life. I remember the way her voice changed when she heard mine on the phone, like she was really, *so* glad to hear my voice. I remember what she'd order over and over again when we'd go out for lunch at our favorite restaurant. I remember her favorite colors, the way she'd wrinkle her nose when she didn't like something, the way her beautiful eyes would cloud when she didn't want to hear what I had to say, the animated ways she had when she was talking about her hopes and dreams. Heather was honest with me, because that's the way it was with us. She chose me, for some reason, as confidante. I was her "other mother," the one she talked to about the hard stuff she couldn't talk to her parents about.

There are things we can never understand in life and one of them that hurts the most is when we lose something precious that we'll never regain. One of them that we can never understand is a life cut short, the loss of a child. A parent should never have to bury a child. It's all wrong—it's backwards. Heather was taken away from us at age 27, and we are left to do the best we can and to hang on with all our might to the words, "Peace I leave with you; My peace I give to you; not as the world gives do I give to you. Do not let your heart be troubled . . ." (John 14:27). How do those who don't have Jesus cope without Him?

Although it is almost a year later, we are barely coping. Her parents are so devastated. She leaves two little girls, ages 9 and 3. The 3-year-old scarcely understands that "Mommy went to heaven," although for the 9-year-old it is much harder. They will grow up without her. They will survive, we will survive. But Heather is at peace. Why did this happen?

One thing that comes out of it is this telling. There are just some things we can never understand. Heather had such a huge gift of music—a real, true *gift*. She blessed so many people with her ability to lead others into God's presence in worship. I love music so much myself and when I listen to it, so many songs remind me of Heather. I think of the ones I heard her sing; certain voices remind me of her. Then there are even certain other voices that she didn't care for, so *those* make me think of her too. I can envision her on stage singing, I remember her as a little girl holding a microphone almost as large as her little forearm. I remember holding her in my arms as she wept because she didn't think she sang well enough (she was always *so* good!). I remember struggling through Christmas productions that were so difficult to stage and feeling they were so inadequate because the outcome didn't match my vision of what I wanted to do to glorify my God and reach the lost—then having Heather's music being the one really *good* thing in it, and thinking, "This song has saved the Christmas production for me and made all the work worthwhile." Then, this past Christmas I was almost not able to bear my grief because I'd never hear Heather sing *that one song* again. Then when our church staged the children's production, I had to get up and leave because I was sitting alone and I couldn't bear all my memories of Heather as a little girl singing, as a teen singing, as a young woman singing, with no one there to help me bear it and my grief was so fresh. All through the holidays I was grieving and there was no one to help me and comfort me; my husband was away and I grieved alone. Jesus was my only and sole comfort. Almost a year later as I review this I am finally able to cope a little better. It's getting easier, but I don't understand it any better.

I particularly don't understand myself, how I allowed weeks, months, and then over two years to pass since I called this beloved girl of mine—just let the time slip by. I let many relationships slip away like that through the busyness of life.

The Bible even reminds us not to do this, to love one another, to seek each other out: "… *not forsaking our own assembling together, as is the habit of some, but encouraging one another . . ."* (Hebrews 10:25).

How could I let seventeen years of love and relationship pass away like that? My love for her never ended, but I let the expression of it wane, and it all ended with a kiss on a cold forehead when I bent over her in her casket. Does Heather see my tears from heaven as Jesus wipes away her tears (Revelation 21:4)? I wear a special ring I gave her many years ago that her mother Sue returned to me for a keepsake. It will always serve as a daily reminder that she lived in my life—*and* a reminder that God took her away and that sometimes things happen that we don't understand. It's also a reminder that God is always with us, even in the "valley of the shadow of death"—always right at hand, always.

But this I do understand: Heather suffered many things in her life that only those closest to her knew, and now she is at peace. This helps me with my grief. The other thing that helps me is that I did enjoy seventeen years with her and that I will have eternity with her, when I will see her again. One day I'll see her in the kingdom of God, and she won't have to confide the things that are giving her pain, the things she can't discuss with her parents, for those things will all be past. Instead we'll discuss the joy of the LORD. One day we'll sing and worship together, and that's one thing I *do* understand.

Just seven and a half months before Heather's death, we lost another beloved girl, Faith Taber, in whose memory this book is dedicated. Faith, my husband George's niece, died at the age of thirteen of heart failure. She was out with her brother, sister, and her Mom, Linda roller skating and acting like a kid, and when she was about to get into the family van afterwards, she passed out. Linda leapt out and tried to revive her. 911 was called and Faith was taken to the hospital, but she was gone—just like that. No forewarning, no prior illness, no symptoms or complaints—nothing. Faith was called home to be with Jesus that day. Thus we lost not one, but two dearly beloved girls from our family in 2005. It was hard to understand this sudden trauma, this loss of our girl Faith. Why, Lord?

Maybe it is a little easier for Linda and Mark than for Dave and Sue. Heather's parents lost their only child. Linda and Mark, Faith's parents, still have Faith's brother, Mark, Jr., and sister, Hope—that's at least something for them. Further, Faith was younger. She had not yet embarked on an adult life, had not yet started a family of her own. I cannot say that she had not yet begun a ministry, for one might say that of a youth, but those who were present at her memorial service know better; young Faith touched so many lives with her great show of faith and love. Her sweet, quiet spirit and love of God touched many lives and no one knew just how many until people began to stand and share how much Faith's presence had meant in their lives.

As for me, I will always remember Faith's sweet voice, how she would call me up at George's Mom's house when we went to town. Faith would always call too early in the morning, anxious for contact and say, "Aunt Jean, what will we do today?" It was my habit to get together with her and her brother and sister and do something special—just to spend some time together. Often the projects I chose were too ambitious to complete successfully, but the time spent was good—it fostered relationship in the short time I had to spend with them and that accomplished the goal I had in mind: to let them know that they were special to me. Because of these times, I will always remember Faith's voice saying, "Aunt Jean … what will we do?" and remember the special times we had. I'll never hear that voice, that question, again—until that same eternity when I'll see Heather and so many others I'm now parted from.

Just a week before Faith died I had looked at her cell phone number on my bulletin board as I had so many times before and thought, "Wouldn't she be thrilled to get a phone call from out of state?" and I did not call her. Such regrets. Was that a chance from God, a special prompting, to say goodbye to that beloved niece? I can't know, but I can regret that I did not make that phone call. I had another prompting, the week before Heather died, to call *her*. And guess what? I didn't do it. I believe that God gave me a special little nudge each time—a distinct privilege to say goodbye to these loved ones, and I ignored those promptings and failed to receive a blessing.

So I sit here and think of the people I *can* call now and make it a point to keep relationships intact, and when I think of someone to call, to write, to say a special prayer for when they enter my mind—I do it *now* instead of putting it off, instead of letting the prompting pass by. For all the things I *don't* understand, this I *do* understand.

I have also been thinking so much lately of several people in particular that I am close to and the severe trials they seem to suffer continually. Their entire lives seem to be one battle upon another. I think about all I've written about faith and I hope they will read this and somehow find some comfort in it—maybe even some help in it. Then I think how blessed my life is. How do these, my sorely tried loved ones keep on? They are weary and I feel as though I should stop everything and just spend all my time begging God to send them relief. Some of them work so hard, yet they find no financial relief. Some are so sick constantly they can't even work anymore. How do we answer trials of faith like this? I know them to have faith, yet they do not appear to be victorious. So, that must be what it is: the victory is within their souls. Maybe the victory is that they *keep on*—they persevere in the face of all odds. I know that one person in particular is an inspiration to me in that he keeps on in spite of the way things look.

Again I read over my words—read these words I have written and I hope they will bring some comfort, some relief, then upon rereading them I think they sound simplistic, trivial. But how can they be? They are God's own words and they've worked for me. Oh, Lord God! Help my loved ones! They suffer so! So I resolve to pray more, wishing God would take some of my blessings and share them around to these loved ones of mine who suffer so. What is the difference in their lives and mine? Why do I get so many blessings and their lives are so tormented? I can't come up with an answer and I wish I could. It's simply something I can't understand. I have to accept, by faith, that God is there holding them up, bringing them through.

There are instances in the Bible of Jesus doing things we just don't understand. For example, in Mark 11, just after Jesus' triumphal entry into Jerusalem, He passed a fig tree when He was hungry and, finding no figs on it (it not being the season for figs) He cursed it saying, "May no one ever eat fruit from you again" (Mark 11:14). The Bible also says, "And his disciples heard Him say it."

We read this and we think, why did our gentle Jesus do that? Was He just being human—tired and frustrated? Surely a tree without fruit out of season was not unusual. Jesus went on from there to the temple where He threw out the merchants who were selling doves for sacrifices, maybe cheating or short-changing people. Maybe He was a little stressed before that event, knowing what He had to do in the temple? He *was* a man, after all—human. We don't know, but we might think about these things from our own perspective.

The next day, says the Scripture (Mark 11:21), on their return trip, Jesus and the disciples see the fig tree again and see that it has withered away.

Jesus tells His disciples then, "'Have faith in God … I tell you the truth, if anyone says to this mountain, "Go and throw yourself into the sea," and does not doubt in his heart but believes that what he says will happen, it will be done for him. Therefore I tell you, whatever you ask for in prayer, believe that you have received it, and it will be yours. And when you stand praying, if you hold anything against anyone, forgive him, so that your Father in heaven may forgive you your sins. But if you do not forgive, neither will your Father Who is in heaven forgive your sins.'" (Mark 11:22–26).

So maybe that was it. Maybe the whole point of the curse upon that tree was for a lesson to the disciples. Something that we think Jesus may have done in passing was actually something very serious. God does not do things lightly. He is always watching us, always teaching us, even when we don't know what the purpose is of the things He does. So when you don't understand, wait and watch. God has a purpose for all these things in your life. He is faithful; He will show you what is happening soon enough. There are reasons—and if not to teach you something, there are reasons enough for what has happened. The reasons, while they are not necessarily to our benefit, may be God's alone and we just have to trust Him.

Recharging Your Faith

*"Let us fix our eyes on Jesus, the author and perfector of our faith,
Who for the joy set before Him endured the cross scorning its
shame, and sat down at the right hand of God."*

—Hebrews 12:2

Day by day we walk with God and grow in our faith and
trust of Him. We do the best we can and hope for the best.
Our faith grows and we have hope because of our faith.
Sometimes our lives are wonderful and things are great, but
sometimes things are really miserable in spite of our faith
and we wonder what has happened. Some may say "the ceil-
ing is made of brass," an expression used to indicate that
they feel their prayers are going nowhere, that they don't
sense God's presence, that their faith is perhaps in some
measure wavering. So what is the answer?

We move from day to day exercising our faith and it
grows and develops like a muscle. But even the strongest,
best-developed muscles have off days, the healthiest bodies
sometimes succumb to illness. So do the strongest in faith
sometimes suffer trials of their faith and doubt their God.
Sometimes it is merely a fleeting thought, sometimes it is a
season of deep despair. We read in the Bible that one of the
apostles, Thomas, one who walked with Christ and knew

Him personally, said that he doubted that Jesus had died and risen again.

"Show me," Thomas said, asking to see the nail prints in Jesus' hands and feet, "then I'll believe it" (John 20:24–28).

We think, "How could Thomas have doubted the reports of Christ after all the miracles he had seen, after all he knew about Christ?" But we weren't there during that tumultuous time. We didn't know what Thomas had been through, what was happening in his heart, mind, and spirit. We don't know how we would have responded in similar circumstances.

There's a little saying that goes: "When you point a finger at someone else there are three pointing back at you."

So true. Don't consider how someone else is lacking in faith, until you consider how you may feel when your own faith wavers. So what shall we do when our faith is low? You may find yourself hiding, rolled up in a blanket in the dark, avoiding even people you are close to. Maybe that's not a bad thing; for it may be what you need to do to recover from something devastating, something that has wounded you so deeply that there is no other way to recover. Perhaps you are too sick at heart, too troubled in your spirit to do anything at all other than to simply wait at Jesus' feet, to simply be embraced by our Father as the hurt ebbs little by little. Maybe this is not a trial of your faith at all, but just a waiting until things in your world right themselves. Some things can only be cured by time and nothing else, such as the loss of a beloved one, or something equally devastating that you simply cannot grasp. For these things there is nothing that can be done other than to wait. Your spirit can only overcome in the waiting, for God will heal you in time; thus you must cling to Him and wait for the time to pass, for it surely will in due course. The pain and devastation will not last forever, although it may seem now as if it surely will.

Sometimes it is an anger in your spirit that you are dealing with. I remember one sore trial that I suffered. I had been very ill for several years and was in a great deal of pain. I spent several years in bed, many months confined to a barren bedroom because I was so chemically sensitive that I couldn't come out of there. I had to be fed intravenously to stay alive and lived life in a sort of fog. I couldn't even have books or papers, for I was even allergic to them. During this time, a friend of mine died suddenly after having triumphed several times over cancer. The cancer had returned abruptly, metastasized, and taken her life before the doctors realized what was happening. She was a single mother, a Christian, and left behind two elementary-age children.

I was very angry with God because He had taken Sheila away, had taken her to heaven. I didn't understand why He had deprived the children of their mother, first of all, but that wasn't what angered me. What I resented was that *she* got to go to heaven while *I* was still bound to earth.

"What do I have to do," I demanded of God, "to get off this earth?" Then I heard my own voice say out loud, "What do I have to do to go to heaven?" and I started to cry, because I knew the answer, and the answer is Jesus. There is no other answer. I won't be going until God is finished with me here on earth.

Of course it sounds silly and absurd now. But at the time it was a sore trial for me. I was very sick and I wanted to go to heaven. I wanted to quit earth and be done with life. Why, I demanded, did Sheila get to go, and not me? *Why* did I have to stay here on earth and be sick and in pain and miserable—and why did she get to quit and go to heaven? *Why??* After weeping and demanding that of God,

I was so angry I couldn't speak to Him for two days. I was miserable, for when you are a Christian in a room alone with no one to talk to but God, you spend a *lot* of time with Him. Eventually I overcame my bitterness and humbled myself and asked His forgiveness for my foolishness and was restored, but it was a sad time for me. The final outcome of the situation was that He *healed* me. That's why *I* didn't get to go to heaven! I know, looking back, that this was a case of faith worn so thin from such a long, long battle that I just sort of fell apart. I was so sick physically and so sick with disappointment and longing so for relief that I couldn't see beyond it. Now when I look back I can better see what was driving that unreasonableness, that childish little tantrum. But God understood the whole while.

Perhaps when your faith is low you turn your attention elsewhere. Maybe you turn your focus to something such as work, and immerse yourself deeply—so deeply you don't have time for anything else. Then you find you are tired—more tired than you've ever felt before, probably as a result of such a rigorous schedule. You are overtired, too stressed to go on. Your devotional life, your prayer time, meditation, then church attendance and fellowship all gradually fall by the wayside. There is no time for the things of God and you suddenly find yourself far from God Himself—and this is a very bad thing. When we are avoiding God, we are hiding from the only One Who can help us back onto the path of recovery. Maybe it's this very pressure that took you to the trial you are in in the first place. If one is under excessive pressure constantly, it is time to pull back for a while when suffering exhaustion. Pressure can be a good thing. Pressure can form a beautiful diamond. But pressure can also crush strong bones and level a village under an avalanche. It depends on the amount and type of pressure we're talking about. Pressure can be like boulders in a stream—arranged properly, the water can tumble around them and be purified, but arranged differently they can dam the water causing it to cease to flow. So it is with our spirits. If the pressure is too much and the wrong kind, it can destroy. If it is right and good, it can form us into something beautiful, pure, and good. How then can we make use of this pressure to make something good and fine of us, rather than allowing it to crush and destroy us? First let us draw near to God, to hide ourselves in Him, and let Him release the pressure.

Psalm 32:7 says, "You are my hiding place; You preserve me from trouble . . ."

II Chronicles 15:2 says, "the LORD is with you when you are with Him. And if you seek Him, He will let you find Him. . . ."

For myself, these promises bear up. I have never gone seeking God and come away not having found Him. God is always there for you. If you come away from seeking Him without finding Him, go back, for He is there. He will rescue you, so do not be dismayed.

If something has happened to separate you from God, you need to be restored. If you are right, you will be vindicated; if you are wrong you will be forgiven and restored when you turn back to God and make things right with Him and with any other person involved. Father will help you; do not be afraid to go to Him.

There are so many ways to build ourselves back up. Consider how Christ endured such strong opposition from sinful men "so you will not grow weary and lose heart" (Hebrews 12:3).

Of course, we say, He was God. But we must remind ourselves that He laid aside Heaven. He laid aside His deity and came to earth as a man, to live among men and bear everything we do in order to understand our griefs and sorrows, to live as we do. He was rejected as a man, He suffered as we do, and far beyond anything we do, for He suffered separation from God when He was on the cross, and when He descended into hell, something we will never have to do.

This was why Jesus cried out, "My God, My God, why have you forsaken Me?" God had to turn away from Jesus when He bore all the sins of the world, for God, being holy, cannot bear sin. So let's look at how Jesus "recharged," how He overcame temptation, and got back on His feet and went on again, day by day.

In the book of Hebrews, the apostle Paul admonishes us to "endure hardships as discipline" as this helps us grow in righteousness and produces a life of peace: "It is for discipline that you endure; God deals with you as with sons; for what son is there whom his father does not discipline?" (Hebrews 12:7)

He reminds us that if God did not care for us, He would not bother to shape us constantly through discipline. Why would He bother to continue to train us if He did not care about us, His dear children? He would simply ignore us and allow us to go our sinful ways.

While I have been working on this book I have, of necessity, spent so very much time in the Word and in prayer—more than ever before in my life—as well as time quietly meditating and reflecting on what God is trying to teach us. During these periods, I also listen to Christian music and spend much more time worshipping and praising God than at any other time.

Psalm 16:11 says, "You will make known to me the path of life; in Your presence is fullness of joy; in Your right hand there are pleasures forever."

Sometimes entire days and nights at a time are given over to the LORD and this work, and then something very special happens. It is as though I have entered a world apart and it is then that I have a special glimpse of where and how it is that God truly wants His children to walk with Him. While we are here on earth we must endure the world, but we can still commune with God for we carry Him always within ourselves when we truly belong to Him. We are of the world yet not of the world, set apart—in a separate world within ourselves with God. This belonging to God is a different place within us, a special condition of the soul that keeps us fit for things that those who do not know God and His ways are not.

When Jesus finished ministering He would withdraw to pray (Matthew 14:23, Mark 6:46). He rarely allowed anything to interfere with this, although sometimes this couldn't be helped, as when someone who desperately needed Him pressed in and called to Him. Sometimes our quiet times fall by the wayside because life calls too loudly, but we must set aside time to rest and seek the LORD. If *Jesus* needed quiet time, how can *we* manage without?

"Submit therefore to God," says James 4:7. But consider this second critical part too: *"Resist the devil and he will flee from you."*

If we are not submitted to God, close to Him, we are not prepared to fight the enemy. Jesus demonstrated this strength in fasting and prayer during His forty days in the wilderness.

"Draw near to God," says James 4:8, "and He will draw near to you."

So let us draw near—very near. Let us begin the day with God, and end the day with God. Let us fortify ourselves with the Scriptures in the morning and be vitalized for the day, and start out clean and fresh. Let us end the day in peace saying good night to our Father, thanking Him for bringing us through—a *real* "nightcap."

Despite even this closeness, we will still be tried. We should not be surprised at the trials we will suffer, for they are common to the people of God. We are in a spiritual war. The rewards for these trials are more precious than "gold which is perishable" (I Peter 1:6–7). These trials are for honoring God, for developing in us a holiness that fits us for the kingdom, that makes us more God-like, "like the Holy One Who called us" (I Peter 1:15). When we know this, it is easier to bear these trials, to work through them and to come out on the other side standing tall rather than stooped by exhaustion, bent and broken by a heavy burden. Sometimes the burden *is* heavy but our help is right at hand—even when we feel we can't bear up. Sometimes we are too numb to pray—that's why it's so important to pray when we are able and to have the Word embedded within. Then when the trials come, we cry out by an instinct that we have by this closeness we've developed with God.

Even Jesus was sometimes overwhelmed. "'My soul,'" He said, "'is overwhelmed with sorrow to the point of death'" (Matthew 26:29, NIV).

Sometimes we find ourselves needing a recharging of our faith because we have simply lost our focus. The world presses in and we get too busy. We start piling one thing on top of another until we are weary of it all. I hope that my loved ones can remain focused on God, but how can they, for they must be so weary? How can I possibly encourage them?

Recently my busy brother Bob decided to trade something he's been doing for years to take on a ministry at church as a better service to God, a better use of his time and talents. This is a beautiful example of what God wants His people to do. Re-evaluate your life periodically to make sure you're still doing what God wants for that time in your life. Just because something has always been right and has always fit, doesn't mean it will continue so. God can direct us to better ways. There was really nothing wrong in what he was doing—he is just more useful where he now is. Sometimes we need the courage to tear ourselves away from what we're doing and start fresh in something brand new.

I Peter 5:8–9 says, "Be self-controlled and alert. Your enemy the devil prowls around like a roaring lion looking for someone to devour. Resist him, standing firm in your faith, knowing that the same experiences of suffering are being accomplished by your brethren who are in the world."

This makes me contemplate the suffering of Christ's martyrs of today, for there are indeed many. We don't think of them often enough as we live our privileged lives in America. Here, we suffer little for Christ's Name. In many countries, particularly Muslim lands, to champion Christ's name is to die.

Pay attention to what your schedule is like. Re-analyze it periodically and see whether it is appropriate for a child of God. Does it serve God first, then your family? Does it leave you with some margins so you're not always running behind? Do you have time for God and your loved ones? Do you have time for yourself, time to decompress and rest? In this way you can recharge your faith by always being a step ahead. In this way you will be able to keep your faith recharged before your spiritual batteries run down. In this way the enemy will be in front of you where you can keep an eye on him and not behind you where he can sneak up on you. In this way you will know what God wants for you, and not have to be guessing whether you are on the right path.

If you are overscheduled, overcommitted, and overtired, do something about it. Too many people today are stressed out and don't sleep well. It's becoming a common problem, almost a national epidemic. If you have this problem, do something about it.

God wants you to be able to sleep. God even has specific promises for this in Psalm 4:8, "In peace I will both lie down and *sleep*, for You alone, O LORD, make me to dwell in safety . . ." and in Psalm 3:5, "I lay down and *slept*; I awoke, for the LORD sustains me."

As you walk with God, do not be surprised if you are not the most popular person around because of your open, candid commitment to Him. However, be sure that it is not a judgmental or "holier-than-thou" attitude that makes this so. Others may avoid you, shun you, even hate you because of your love for Christ, but make sure it's your pure love of and service to Him (I John 3:13). Knowing this will help you keep things in perspective. Don't let your faith suffer because of the way you are treated by those who don't know and understand God and the things of God. We who are born of God have the power to overcome the things of the world. God's commandments are not burdensome to those who love God. It is only that we tire from the onslaught of the battle, like any soldier on any battlefield (I John). We just need our rest. It's so critical to remember that. We can't go on and on. We are *not* "Energizer bunnies." I've had to learn the hard way that I can't constantly push my limits and expect to keep going. I will—literally—drop if I do.

Consider this: "This is the confidence we have before Him, that, if we ask anything according to His will, He hears us. If we know that He hears us in whatever we ask, we know that we have the requests which we have asked from Him" (I John 5:14–15).

So because of this wonderful truth—that we can have *anything* we ask from our wonderful God—we must "build ourselves up" in our faith. We must pray in the Holy Spirit, waiting for that coming answer (Jude 1:20). If He will bring us eternal life, will He leave us miserable waiting for it? I think not.

I love this psalm: "Let me hear Your lovingkindness in the morning; for I trust in You; teach me the way in which I should walk; for to You I lift up my soul" (Psalm 143:8).

Escape your situation. Get away from it. You can't gain perspective from the midst of your chaos. Lift your heart up to God and He will comfort you. The Holy Spirit is the greatest Comforter of all. Put on good music and praise and worship God, for your soul and spirit are crying out for God.

> *"As a deer pants for the water, so my soul pants for You, O God. My soul thirsts for God, for the living God. Where can I go to meet God?"*
>
> *(Psalm 42:1–2).*

Eat some good food—not junk, but something nutritious and wholesome, maybe different or even exotic—whether you cook it for yourself or go out. Call someone you haven't talked to for a long time, or go visit a good friend. Get some rest when you are disheartened and discouraged. Take a nap if you can. Take a vacation, if even for a few hours or a half day. Take off and take your mind off your troubles with play. Find things that make you lighthearted, that produce laughter, such as a funny movie or book. I love finding children to play with. Jesus Himself found delight in children.

Go to a place of sheer beauty and enjoy God's magnificent creation. For me, there is no better way to recharge than this, especially coupled with magnificent music. Recently

I was invited to a concert when I was very tired. I went because I knew the music would be a much better restorative than sleep could ever be.

"Teach me to do Your will, for You are my God; let Your good Spirit lead me on level ground" (Psalm 143:10).

I want my walk to be straight and true, and this is how I can do it. I don't want to stumble along, I don't want to fall down and scrape myself up. I don't want to be fumbling along in the dark all the time, so I let God lead me along. I have had enough experience with trying to do things mechanically, exhausted spiritually and physically, doing a marginal job of it all. This is not what God wants from us or for us.

> "The LORD is faithful to all His promises and loving toward all
> He has made"
>
> *(Psalm 145:13, NIV).*

God is always there for us. He never turns away. Never. From Jesus, He turned away. Jesus had to bear that, just as He had to bear all the sins of the world. Jesus had to bear the ultimate loneliness, the abandonment of God. This is how Jesus experienced the loss of the soul abandoned in hell. God would never abandon us, His children, like that; He has so much more for us.

> "The LORD your God is in your midst, a victorious warrior. He
> will exult over you with joy ... He will rejoice over you with
> shouts of joy"
>
> *(Zephaniah 3:17).*

God will *exult* over us when we are victorious. Can you envision Him saying to His Son and to the angels, "Look! She's one of mine! See? Victorious!"

We must have periods of renewal, crying out to God, seeking Him and waiting on Him. But it is not always that easy. It is not always just waiting for Him to rescue us. There is something we must do too. While we are waiting we must humble ourselves. We must wait, we must *confess our sins.*

I Peter 2:1 tells us how to prepare to call on God. "So be done with every trace of wickedness (depravity, malignity) and all deceit and insincerity (pretense, hypocrisy) and grudges (envy, jealousy) and slander and evil speaking of every kind" (Amplified Version).

In other words, get down on your knees and give your conscience a thorough going-over. This is not just about God ministering to us, it is about us examining ourselves and the way we have been living, about ridding ourselves of sin.

"The LORD is righteous in all His ways," says Psalm 145:17.

So we must confess our sins before we can bask in the presence of the LORD. God does not leave us, even when we sin, because He says we belong to Him. Even when we do not sense His presence, He is there waiting for us because He says He will never leave us or forsake us (I Kings 8:57). He is faithful to us, He is there for us. We do not have to doubt Him ever. He is ever faithful. God will rescue us in our time of need, always—*always.* If we are right, God will come to our rescue. If we are wrong, God will still come to our rescue when we are ready to repent and come back to Him. It doesn't matter. He is always ready for us, always waiting for us. Always, *always.* This part is so hard for me, because I continually realize just how much sin there is in my life. How can God put up with me? But He keeps His promises still! It is true that He will discipline us, but He must; that is what a loving parent does with his children. How else will we learn? We must accept that, for how else can we grow? But when it is over, there we are, back in the center of God's love.

He doesn't ask for elaborate sacrifices: "For You do not delight in sacrifice, otherwise I would give it; You are not pleased with burnt offering. The sacrifices of God are a broken spirit; a broken and a contrite heart, O God, You will not despise" (Psalm 51:16–17).

So I come, after confessing my sins and ask God again, "Create in me a pure heart, O God, and renew a right spirit within me. Do not cast me from your presence or take Your Holy Spirit from me. Restore to me the joy of Your salvation and grant a willing spirit, to sustain me" (Psalm 51:10–12).

I make it my prayer again and again. It is our humility in realizing our sinfulness that God finally honors. It is our humility that brings us to the place of forgiveness. *It is our pride that has taken us to the place of sin, but it is our humility that has taken us home to God again.*

"When pride comes, then comes dishonor, but with the humble is wisdom"

(Proverbs 11:2).

So let us remember humility when God has cleansed us and taken us back again.

I spent many years moving from one area of ministry to another as God led me. Even when I was quite ill it seemed there was always something I felt God wanted me to do. I'm not certain I was always supposed to be doing it, but I felt I was supposed to at the time. Then, suddenly, I was replaced in an area I truly loved. I was stricken, for I truly loved the ministry I was in and I didn't understand why I was being replaced. I felt truly bereft, and I was miserable. I went through a period of mourning and I couldn't talk to anyone about it, for it was a decision made by a ministry department head and I really had no say about it. I couldn't discuss it with anyone, for all my friends were in ministry and it would be disloyal to discuss it with anyone—to talk about it might constitute gossip.

I was numb with grief because I did not understand. The pastor who removed me from that ministry had other plans for me, but neglected to tell me that. I was dismayed at being removed, for I was very happy doing what I was doing and didn't want to do anything else, thinking I was "too old" (my goodness, 50!) to start something else, even though it turned out to be something I had shown interest in in the past. Others I had worked with came and asked why I had "quit" and I had no answer not only because I had not quit, but because I didn't understand what was going on. All I could do was weep, and I did it privately because I had no one to talk to—except Jesus. Jesus was all I had and it was to Him I went.

During this time I would awake in the morning crying. When I went to sleep at night, I was weeping. I wept at odd times during the day when I prayed. I had lost my ministry and my friends, for all my friends were in that ministry. But for Jesus, I would have been alone—and so I clung to Jesus and I clung *hard*. I was very literally in mourning, for I had lost the fellowship of many friends and a way of life I loved. My friends were all busy in the ministry I had left and was no longer a part of; when they were meeting, I was no longer among them. I simply clung to Jesus and grieved for what I had lost; He was my only and sole solace and comfort.

Now when I look back and I think about that time I wonder what I would have done without Jesus. How could I have survived that trauma? I went to the doctor for some odd illness or another and he asked me how I was and when I told him what had happened he was appalled. I was a *volunteer* and I was *fired*. (This was how I—however wrongly—

perceived it.) I did finally get things in perspective; I truly wasn't fired—I was meant to move into another area and there was instead miscommunication and misunderstanding on my part.

All of this was very sad and I was unhappy, and I chose a sabbatical instead of changing ministries, but that's not the point. My husband traveled and was not home much and so couldn't comfort me, and as it is, men aren't great with tears. But there is one Man Who is, and one Friend Who carried me through when I couldn't talk about it to the many friends I had lost fellowship with. The point is that I did have *Someone* to hold me, comfort me, and take me through a deep, deep trauma. Jesus is always there, *always*. I don't know how I could get by without Him. He's proved to be the only One reliable all the time throughout the last 29 years of my life. My husband is wonderful and I love him deeply. I have a big loving family, including my in-laws who don't fit the stereotypical in-law jokes, some very dear and kind friends, but they can't always be right there for me because they have lives too. We are all, after all, human and fall short of the ideal. We'll never be good enough to hold each other up and be wonderful enough to help each other through all of the traumas of this life. Only Jesus is perfect all the time. But we do try to love each other, and that's important. You can find some of that "recharging" in other Christians. Jesus Himself found some consolation in fellow man when He walked the earth. If He felt the need of friends, we should follow His example and reach out to others when we are in need as well.

So, remember when you feel off course that you are not alone. When you feel low, when you feel your faith is weak, remember that you are part of a large body of believers on earth. When you feel you can't reach God, when you feel He is very far away, other believers are only a phone call away. Get in touch with them and they will help you get in touch with the Father, the Son and the Holy Spirit. We are all in this life on earth together, all straining together to get to our Father up above. You are never alone. If you feel you *are* alone, you have only to contemplate this Scripture:

"No temptation has overtaken you but such as is common to man; and God is faithful Who will not allow you to be tempted beyond what you are able, but with the temptation will provide the way of escape also, so that you will be able to endure it" (I Corinthians 10:13).

Appendix I:
Apologetics

America has come a long way from the days when Christianity was considered as good and noble—or even normal, expedient, useful or practical. It is, in fact, beginning to be viewed with suspicion. When religious fanaticism is the basis for *jihad* (holy war), when abuse is hidden behind the altar screen, when fraud is committed in the name of Jesus, how can anyone fully trust us?

So Christians need to tread softly, to make sure our truths are pure truths indeed. We must make sure we present one face and not two, make sure we bring God to the people who do not know Him, and not instead get in His way. Thus what matters most when we come speaking of Him is what people hear, what they see, what they believe. When we leave those we speak with, what impressions, thoughts, and ideas do we leave behind?

When Jesus walked the earth, the people followed Him, they sought Him out. He tried to get away from time to time, to go off alone and pray, but they scarcely and rarely left Him alone. They dogged His steps, they pressed in upon Him. He was always in the midst of a crowd. He had the real thing, and they knew it. But not everyone was welcoming, not everyone was that eager to be around Him, to hear Him, to embrace Him. Every day He was teaching, healing, ministering, yet many of the Jewish elders wanted no part of Him.

Luke 19:47–48 says, "And He was teaching daily in the temple; but the chief priests and the scribes and the leading men among the people were trying to destroy Him, and they could not find anything that they might do, for all the people were hanging onto every word He said."

They wanted badly to get rid of Jesus, but they couldn't because of the people. He was just too popular and public opinion wouldn't bear it.

These words of His that the people hung on were the eternal truths of Scripture, but the chief priests and elders of the Jewish faith used them as a club to lord it over the people. In answer to their harsh rule, Jesus challenged them with their own teachings and thus provided defense of the pure Word of God, which is what we call "apologetics."

The word apologetics is derived from the Greek word *apologia,* which means to "make a rational defense." The purpose of apologetics is to defend the truth of the Word of God and the deity of Jesus Christ. Jesus did this with the fine points of the law that the chief priest tried to use as riddles to trip Him up (Matthew 22). What Jesus did with the precious Word of God was to take it back from the cold legalistic elders and make it vital and living once again, as God meant it to be. Jesus gave us, instead of dread laws, guidelines to live by. Instead of legalism, love. In return, the self-proclaimed masters of the law sought Jesus' death—and eventually won it.

But this was foreordained, predestined for our salvation, our way in eternity. Instead of a retelling of that story here, let us turn our attention to apologetics.

The apostle Paul cautions us, "Be diligent to present yourself approved to God as a workman who does not need to be ashamed, accurately handling the word of truth" (II Timothy 2:15).

This directs us to study the Word, to be sure of what it says in order to give answer to those who may question us. While we are immersed in the Word and prayer on a regular basis, we can have the confidence that the Holy Spirit will help us to make it such a part of our lives that we will begin to incorporate it in our thought life, and so in our memories and conversation. Still we must prepare ourselves to answer in many other ways. The apostle Paul, we see from our studies, engaged in apologetics in the book of Acts.

Thus should we pursue at least a passing study of apologetics. Basic apologetics are of two kinds. The first asserts that there is One true God; it is used in defense against agnostics, atheists and pantheists, those who do not understand or embrace our God. The second presupposes that there *is* that One true God and then defends the position that God took human form in the Person of Jesus Christ, was born as a child to a virgin, that He was the awaited Messiah, that He ministered here on earth, was crucified, died, and rose again, and will come again. This type of apologetics is used in argument against Judaics who still await a Messiah, against Islamics and against non-evangelical so-called Christians who do not believe in Christ's deity.

Apologetics is the systematic arrangement of knowledgeable answers to questions concerning the truths about historic events that answer the objections of those who pose questions against Christ. Apologetics today is a specific discipline based on studies developed for the defense of truths of Christ's deity and the Bible as the Word of God. There are many books that give extensive treatment to the subject.

Apologetics is said to have had its start in Athens after Christ's death, although Jesus and the apostles clearly engaged in this defense of the Word of God. All Christians should have at least a passing knowledge of apologetics so that they may have an answer to arguments posed against the Word of God and against Christ's deity by non-believers.

The following is a brief list of recommended books, although there are many to choose from readily available both online and at your local Christian bookstore and library. I am particularly familiar with Lee Strobel's and Josh McDowell's work, and find these works to be not only eminently readable but fascinating as well.

The Case for Christ
Lee Strobel
Zondervan 1998
ISBN 0310209307

The Case for Easter
Lee Strobel
Zondervan 2004
ISBN 0310241448

More Than a Carpenter
Josh McDowell
Tyndale House 1977
ISBN 0842345523

New Evidence that Demands a Verdict
Josh McDowell
Thomas Nelson 1999
ISBN 0785242198
Christian Apologetics
Norman L. Geisler

Baker Encyclopedia of Christian Apologetics
Norman L. Geisler
Baker Books 1998
ISBN 0801021510

Pocket Handbook of Christian Apologetics
Peter Kreeft and Ronald Tacelli
Inter-Varsity Press 2003
ISBN 0830827021

Humble Apologetics: Defending the Faith Today
John G. Stackhouse, Jr.
Oxford University Press 2002
ISBN 0195138074

Appendix II: World News

Whatever your politics may be, it is imperative, urgent, and essential that you understand that we fight not against the actual powers that be—the governments of this world—but against the unseen principalities and powers of the spiritual realm. The Bible, besides being everything we need to know about God's perfect will and the road map for a good and successful life, is a book of history and a book foretelling what the future holds both here on earth and in eternity.

Following these few articles of news, I have given a few outstanding examples from the Word that will help to illustrate the awe-inspiring truth of God's Word and how He demonstrates His desire to show Himself. God does not hide Himself in obscurity, but makes plain both the past and what will take place in the future. He shows His will in His commands, demonstrating the impossibility of our ability to achieve His level of holiness, then promises a remedy in the person of the Word made flesh, the Savior, Jesus Christ. He lays out the plan clearly, intertwining it with records of man's victories through obedience to Him, and man's failures through his rebellion against Him. These are not fiction, but recorded in secular history uncovered by painstaking archaeology down through the years.

Today, thousands of years later, we are still the same in our hearts and spirits: weak, though we fight to be strong; ever rebellious, trying to replace God's authority with our own; constantly failing to measure up to His holiness; trying ever to make God less than He is. Is He silent because He has given up on us? But no, He is not silent at all. Instead, He is present in the still, small voice (I Kings 9:12) inside all of us if we will only be still and listen. But He also gives evidence of His being, not only in His creation but also in history through fulfillment of prophecy, and through the very physical evidence of the lives of His people and their history that is left behind, that we may see and be convinced.

Thus do I include this Appendix to enlighten you, perhaps to in some way encourage you, to give you something to hang onto, to grow on, to meditate on.

From Adam to Noah, from Moses to Abraham, God is present both in the Spirit and in the flesh. He walked with Adam and Eve in the Garden of Eden, guided with the pillars of smoke and fire in the desert, supped with Abraham under the tree in Abraham's camp.

And, surprise, the Garden of Eden was in Mesopotamia, the cradle of civilization, in Iraq. That is where Noah built his ark, where his rebellious descendants built the Tower of Babel in their proud bid to reach the heavens. Abraham was born in Ur, in southern Iraq, and it is from Nahor in Iraq that his son Isaac's wife was brought. Isaac's son Jacob, renamed Israel, found his wife Rachel in Iraq. Thus, the seat of Judaism, was Iraq. Yes, God's own chosen people were called forth from the land of one of their bitterest enemies on earth.

Jonah was sent into Iraq—Nineveh—to bring God's Word and warn them of coming destruction. It was in Iraq that Daniel was thrown into the lion's den. Shadrach,

Meshach and Abednego, were thrown into the fiery furnace for their refusal to honor any god but the true God almighty. The mighty Babylon, spoken of so many times in the Bible, is in Iraq. This place figures greatly in the end times.

Belshazzar, the King of Babylon saw the "writing on the wall" (Daniel 5:5) in Iraq, and Nebuchadnezzar, King of Babylon, carried the Jews captive into Iraq. Ezekiel preached in Iraq, as did Peter. In fact, next to Israel, Iraq is the nation most often mentioned in the Bible, although not by that name. Instead, its territories are named: the cities of Babylon, Shinar, Mesopotamia (translated as "between two rivers," these two being the Tigris and Euphrates). There is no other country with more prophecy associated with it than Iraq—except Israel.

There is another country mentioned too: the symbol of that country is the eagle—the United State's own symbol. Other countries that are mentioned throughout the Old Testament by symbol are Russia (the bear), Germany (the leopard), Judah/Israel (the lion) and Greece (the ram). The Old Testament is rich in symbolism and one can learn much about what is to come in the future. Why then do so many seek instead to search star charts and consult mediums and horoscopes? Laziness? Desire for intrigue? Apparently they have no idea how intriguing the Scriptures are. The enemies of Christianity, the Muslims, are fierce and know their books well and can quote them. Christians should take a lesson from this.

On the other hand, the leaders of Muslim lands who seek to destroy the United States would do well to not only read what is written in the Bible (and consider its success rate) but also heed its own prophecy in the Koran (the Islamic bible) that says:

"For it is written that a son of Arabia would awaken

a fearsome Eagle. The wrath of the Eagle would be felt throughout the lands of Allah and lo, while some of the people trembled in despair still more rejoiced; for the wrath of the Eagle cleansed the lands of Allah; and there was peace" Koran (9:11).

In our need to believe all religion is good, most of us think that Muslims benefit from religion as we do, which is not true. We think, as Christians, that living close to one's god will make everyone gentler, calmer, more loving, more peaceful, more principled. But it's not so with Muslims.

Reader, if you say I am an Islamophobe (frightened of Muslims), this is true; if you are not, you may be shortly. Perhaps you aren't grasping the truth of what is yet. Let me share some more of what I know, then ask you to read the newspapers and listen a little more to the news. Islam is directed to "kill the infidel"; anyone who does not believe in the religion of Islam, who does not practice Islam, is an "infidel." They mean you great harm, Christian, for you are an "infidel," and you are their enemy and to be disposed of. Do you understand that now? Read the following excerpts and learn a little more.

Islamic Culpability by Vernon Richards, FaithFreedom. org—(Isralert.com source: Thanks to Israeli Intelligence Maven Bruce Tefft) "…As we fight terrorists, we have been unable to face the stark reality that Islam, and the example of their revered prophet, are the chief motivation behind various terrorist foot-soldiers. It's not a 'culture,' it's not a few deviants, it's not a government or nation, it's the religion. As we look first one way, and then the other, in-your-face Muslim leaders and lay continue their Jihad against us, pushing their young men to commit acts of inhumane brutality in the name of their hateful god Allah. … surrounding a philosophy calling itself a religion, hell-bent on murdering or enslaving the rest of humanity… The 9/11 hijackers, the London Bombers, the Beslan child-killers, the Chechen terrorists, the Palestinian terrorists, the Madrid terrorists, the Darfur killers, the Iraqi murderers, The Bali bombers, and innumerable acts of murder and carnage, are all linked. The common linkage, is that the victimizers are all devout Muslims! Yes, that wonderful 'religion of peace' we have been so careful to respect. And while the foot-soldiers act to weaken western influence and institutions, 'moderate Islam' continues to do what it does best, hide militants living amongst them and silently cheer from the sidelines. The common denominator in this equation of violence is ISLAM. The common script for all these violent plays is the Qur'an [Koran], the Sira and the Hadith collection. The identical characters for all these ugly occurrences are devout Muslims well steeped in Islamic verse and prose.

"In our need to believe all religion is good, we continue to place blame everywhere else, anywhere else, even ourselves, except where it is due. Naïve to the methods and history of Islam, most of us transfer our own religious experience onto undeserving Muslims, incorrectly assuming that going to the Mosque and more prayer will dissuade Muslims from acts of evil, when it works exactly the opposite. Whereas most religionists leave their places of worship more docile, reflective, and less likely to do harm to others, in Islam worshipers leave the Mosques on Friday and go on murderous riots to avenge some perceived slight. Never, NEVER, encourage a disturbed Muslim to read the Qur'an, or go to a mosque and pray…"

CNN-July 20, 2005: Father of 9/11 hijacker Mohammed Atta warns of 50-year war. The father of one of the September 11 hijackers said today he had no sorrow for what had happened in London and claimed more terrorist attacks would follow. Egyptian Mohamed el-Amir, whose son Mohamed Atta commandeered the first plane that crashed into the World Trade Centre in New York, said there was a double standard in the way the world viewed the victims in London and victims in the Islamic world. El-Amir said the attacks in the US and the July 7 attacks in Britain were the beginning of what would be a 50-year religious war, in which there would be many more fighters like his son. Speaking to a CNN producer in his apartment in the upper-middle-class Cairo suburb of Giza, he declared that terror cells around the world were a 'nuclear bomb that has now been activated and is ticking.' Cursing in Arabic el-Amir also denounced Arab leaders and Muslims who condemned the London attacks as being traitors and non-Muslims. He passionately vowed that he would do anything within his power to encourage more attacks."

The following is an excerpt from a news article from Jerusalem Newswire editorial staff, July 21, 2005: "Security chief reveals staggering terror figures…Israel has been attacked by Palestinian Arab terrorists 25,375 times since October, 2000, General Security Service Director Yuval Diskin told his Knesset overseers Tuesday. That figure includes 142 'suicide' bomb attacks, Diskin said in a briefing to the Knesset Foreign Affairs and Defense Committee. The results of that terrorist onslaught are 1,048 persons murdered and over 5,600 injured and maimed, as well as incalculable mental trauma. Diskin said some 18,000 Palestinian Authority residents and another 225 Arab citizens of Israel have participated in perpetrating these attacks."

Because of these attacks we have seen Israel respond by giving back the Promised Land that has been so hard won. Every inch of ground that they have fought to gain since reoccupying the land since the days of Naziism they are now ceding, giving back, bit by bit in the name of peace as the world stands by. I don't want to get into politics, so instead I will point you back to the Word of God. Jesus wept over Jerusalem and told us to pray for her peace. Will it ever come? I think only when the time of the end, when Jesus comes to rule and reign in the final millennium will there be peace. So pray for the "kingdom to come," for only then will there be peace in Jerusalem.

While all of this goes on around us, America becomes a little more aware that we are truly in danger, for our men and women must fight for liberty. We must protect our shores—we are not as safe as we once were. We are scorned for our prosperity, for our security and wealth. So we must leave our formerly secure shores and go abroad to fight this threat, despite the fact that there is outcry against this here at home.

"Why should we go?" detractors demand. "Why do we have to endanger the lives of Americans on foreign soil?"

I think the threat seems likely enough, given the above. But the threat is not only from without, the threat now is from within as well. We have been compromised, not just from those who have established the threat little by little, by coming and quietly settling among us toward this day, but also because we have been deceived by our enemy, Satan, into thinking that we no longer need God. We are a new society, we are an enlightened society, we are a hardy self-sufficient people. What use have we now for God?

Andy Rooney recently made an enlightening history and civics report about Washington D.C., our great capital, just in case we're ignorant of our roots. A statue of Moses and the Ten Commandments stands atop the U.S. Supreme Court building and on the lower portion of its massive oak doors are carved these same Commandments. As you sit inside the courtroom facing the wall above where the judges sit, you also face those same Ten Commandments.

The very first Supreme Court Justice, John Jay, said: "Americans should select and prefer Christians as their rulers."

Throughout that great city, there are Bible verses etched in stone all over the Federal Buildings and Monuments in Washington, D.C. Apparently our forefathers thought that would help our first rulers rule more judiciously.

While a few people are trying to have references to God removed from the Pledge of Allegiance, saying that our nation is not about God, every session of Congress begins with a prayer by a paid preacher, as it has been since 1777.

James Madison, the fourth president, known as "The Father of Our Constitution" made the following statement: "We have staked the whole of all our political institutions upon the capacity of mankind for self-government, upon the capacity of each and all of us to govern ourselves, to control ourselves, to sustain ourselves according to the Ten Commandments of God."

Fifty-two of the 55 founders of the Constitution were members of the established orthodox churches in the colonies.

Patrick Henry, the great patriot most well-known for his ringing statement of "Give me liberty or give me death!" was a founding father of our country who also said, "It cannot be emphasized too strongly or too often that this great nation was founded not by religionists but by Christians, not on religions but on the Gospel of Jesus Christ."

On the aluminum cap atop the Washington monument in Washington, DC, two words are inscribed, although they are tough to see since they face skyward. These two words are over 555 feet high. They are "Laus Deo," the Latin for "Praise be to God."

Today, God is revealing Himself as never before. Just recently a freshwater pool matching the description of one from the gospel of John was found by workmen repairing a sewer pipe in Jerusalem. This is the Pool of Siloam, a freshwater reservoir that was a major gathering place for ancient Jews according to Hershel Shanks, editor of Biblical Archaeology Review, which reported the find August 14, 2005.

"Scholars have said that there wasn't a Pool of Siloam and that John was using 'a religious conceit' to illustrate a point, said New Testament scholar James H. Charlesworth of the Princeton Theological Seminary. "Now we have found the Pool of Siloam ... exactly where John said it was."

"A gospel that was thought to be pure theology is now shown to be grounded in history," he said. The newly discovered pool is less than 200 yards from another Pool of Siloam, this one a reconstruction built between A.D. 400 and 460 by the empress Eudocia of Byzantium, who oversaw the rebuilding of several Biblical sites.

According to history this is the reputed site where Jesus cured a man blind from birth (John 9:1-2). This find is not unique; such archaeological finds are being made on a regular basis more and more often as time marches on.

It is almost as though God is proclaiming, "Pay attention. I'm coming soon. I'm giving you less time and excuse as the days wear on. Pretty soon you'll have no excuse at all for not listening!"

With advanced telecommunications, there cannot be many left on the globe that have not heard the Name of Jesus. Missionaries have reported going into areas that they thought were unreached and learning that the people knew of a "Great Spirit" and His Son. God Incarnate, in the flesh, walking among us is no secret. Those who do not "know" choose not to know. Those who do not know, do not "know" because they stop up their ears and turn away from the truth—it threatens their chosen lifestyle. God does not call us to live in a comfort zone. Living by faith is not easy. Faith itself is simple, the concept itself is simplicity itself, but simple is not the same as easy. And therein lies the challenge. God calls us to tread the "road less traveled." I believe that God is calling out to us, to America the mightiest nation on earth.

"Prepare!" He says.

As a nation, America grieved together on September 11, 2001, when devastation fell upon us in the bombing of the Twin Towers in New York City, the subsequent bombing of the Pentagon, and the foiled hijacking. We understood that we were attacked. Bewildered, we turned to God as a nation, we mourned and prayed. Sickened, we understood that something was required of us. Subdued, we sought our churches and pastors, we fasted and prayed. Over 5 years later, we understand the threat of terrorism much better. It does not quit; the peril continues. We do not know around which corner the enemy will come next. We have made things a little more secure, we sigh a little with relief. Yet the war rages on and we are intimidated. We have locked up some menaces, we seek others still. The threats are real still.

How long will we wage the war? We are warned by Jesus. He told us ahead of time. "You will be hearing of wars and rumors of wars. See that you are not frightened, for those things must take place, but that is not yet the end. For nation will rise against nation, and kingdom against kingdom, and in various places there will be famines and earthquakes. But all these things are merely the beginning of birth pangs…" (Matthew 24:6-8).

We have these other troubles too—the natural disasters—the raging storms and famines all increasing in intensity and frequency. What is next?

> *"Then they will deliver you to tribulation, and will kill you, and you will be hated by all nations because of My name"*
> *(Matthew 24:9).*

Do they not already hate this so-called "Christian nation," these Muslims? Do they not hate the "infidels?" Is the time of Matthew 24:9 upon us?

So prepare. We do not know what tomorrow brings except for one sure thing: *"As for me, I know that my Redeemer lives, and at the last He will take His stand on the earth. Even after my skin is destroyed, yet from my flesh I shall see God" (Job 19:25-26).*

Appendix III: Paganism in Our Homes

"The LORD *God Almighty is the One you are to regard as holy; He is the one you are to fear. He is the one you are to dread."*
—*Isaiah 8:13*

I am writing this in October, a month that always troubles me deeply with its images of ghosts and goblins, witches and vampires, monsters and mischief. Halloween is big business in North America, and when I express the fact that I do not participate in this so-called holiday, I get stares and shocked murmurs. When I led and taught in children's church, I explained the origins of Halloween. Since very few today know the true roots of this event, I will give you a brief history.

Historically, October 31st marked the end of summer and beginning of harvest, an end to growing and a period of death. During this festival called Samhain, the druids (pagans) built huge sacred bonfires to sacrifice crops and animals to their demon gods (I say it plainly). During these sacrifices they wore the skins of the slain animals to supposedly protect them from the evil of ghosts of the dead said to return on this night, for it was thought that the line between life and death was blurred at this time. They kept the bonfires lit through the night for fear that the evil spirits would damage the crops and otherwise cause trouble for them. They made and wore costumes of the skins of the slain animals and their priests prophesied about the year to come. Hence the context of "trick or treat": appease the demons with an offering and no mischief will follow.

The Romans had parallel celebrations which they combined with this Samhain, one of which was Feralia that commemorated the passing of their dead. A second festival was a day to honor the goddess of fruit and trees, Pomona. As Christianity spread into these lands, it became easier for missionaries to incorporate days honoring saints into pagan festivities than to dissuade their converts from holding their pagan festivals. Hence, the pagan druids' festival of Samhain and the Roman holidays of Feralia and to Pomona were blended and became the festival of All-hallowmas Eve and All-hallowmas. Thus the early Christians were encouraged to remember the dead martyrs and their loved ones who had died instead of being persuaded to give up their pagan customs as they should have been. Unfortunately, the mixing of pagan ritual and Christian commemoration became only compromise.

Down through history as well as today, it is on this night each year that witches' covens hold their most sacred celebrations to their pagan gods—complete with blood sacrifice and secret ritual. Witchcraft, you see, is not confined to fairy tales, cartoons and make-believe. It is very real and called by various names such as Wicca, New Ageism and Paganism and no longer hidden. In fact, the religion is very active and continually, actively, and aggressively recruiting.

After one such teaching when I challenged the children

to stand fast against this holiday and refuse to participate (as to do so was to celebrate a festival to the devil), I was approached by an irate parent who told me I had "ruined the holiday" for their family. I was shaken by the vehemence of her anger, but not one iota moved from my insistence that my teaching was correct and that Christians should not participate in this holiday.

When I told my pastor about what had happened, he merely looked at me and said, "Well, you're right, you know."

Before and since that day I have never been afraid to face down anyone who proclaims to be a Christian and to tell them that I do not participate in this holiday and that, further, I esteem it no different than any other day. I simply ignore it. But no, that's not altogether accurate: I pray for the lost on that day. To provide alternate entertainment to prospective trick-or-treaters, I feel, is to allow them an outlet to celebrate something they should distance themselves from altogether, unless to stand firm and proclaim it as wrong.

I can already hear those who read this and have always participated in the event saying, "Well, that's your opinion."

But no. That not only is not my opinion, but it is no "opinion" at all. It is a matter of fact. It is God's commandment and is not open to interpretation or discussion.

From Harry Potter to horoscopes, from the popular TV show "Charmed" to New Ageism, from the tenets of eastern philosophies interwoven in the martial arts and yoga we study for exercise and recreation, our homes embrace spiritualism that is contrary to the teachings of our God. Some play at ouija boards and palm reading, and consider tarot and mediums harmless, misunderstanding that they are participating in demonism and witchcraft. They think that what they do is harmless, that what they participate in is not real, that it is entertainment, as fictional as the scifi and cartoon movies they watch.

Yet the Bible says that these are contrary to God and punishable by His wrath, for He is a jealous God and does not tolerate such infidelity.

"Hear, O my people, and I will warn you—if you would but listen to Me…you shall have no foreign god among you; you shall not bow down to an alien god. I am the Lord your God….But my people would not listen to Me…would not submit to Me. So I gave them over to their stubborn hearts to follow their own devices… . If my people would follow My ways, how quickly would I subdue their enemies and turn My hand against their foes!" (Psalm 81:8-14, NIV)

We are His and He will not share us with His sworn enemy the devil. And sins, like holiness have their own wages, recompense, consequences.

In Jeremiah 2:17-19, God says very simply to Israel, "look around and identify any other nation who has turned from their gods and taken up with other gods."

It simply was not done. No one changed allegiance from one god to another for fear of the wrath to come.

Why had Israel done this to their God, the only God, Who is, after all, the only One Who could even prove His existence? Then He says, "too many of you even flatly refuse to acknowledge and serve Me even though you know Who I am."

Doesn't this seem familiar? It should, for it is the pattern of today. Modern humankind goes blissfully about its business and callously leaves God out of the picture even being so bold as to claim that He has no business being included in our lives, in our schools, in our courts, in our governments—even in the American government that was founded upon His name. (See *Appendix II: World News.*)

Paul warned the Ephesians (4:19) to be careful about compromising their walk saying that living in such a way caused the gentiles to "lose all sensitivity" to God. Ephesians 4:30 warns us not to grieve the Holy Spirit of God, the natural outcome of losing that sensitivity. If we follow a spiritual path that is counter to the purity and holiness of God's nature, counter to His divine nature, how can we remain in step with Him?

What does that mean? Is God grieved by the way we live, blatantly blaspheming His Name, making a mockery of everything holy, a joke of anything that bears His name, using His Holy Name as a casual expletive? Any use of God's Holy Name that is not a prayer, praise, or witness to Him is blasphemy. Are we using witchcraft and sorcery, the power of the enemy as a hobby and a game, using images of gods and goddesses as interior design and body decoration? Yes, indeed, we've lost all sensitivity. It never even occurs to anyone that we've done anything wrong, and if anyone mentions that it might be wrong, we are horrified and scoff at such a ridiculous notion.

But God always offers us saving grace, atonement for everything. He beckons us back time after time.

"If you put your detestable idols out of my sight and no longer go astray…then the nations will be blessed by Him and in Him they will glory"

(Jeremiah 4:1-2).

God calls us back over and over and we do not listen, becoming more and more wicked day by day.

> *"Why has the land been laid waste? The Lord said, 'It is because they have forsaken my law which I set before them; they have not obeyed me or followed my law. Instead they have followed the Baals [idols]. ....I will scatter them...I will pursue them until they have been destroyed'"*
>
> *(Jeremiah 9:12–14).*

Think about this. Israel was once a country with their own rich and flourishing land. Again and again down through recorded history they have disobeyed God and have been scattered across the face of the earth, being taken captive, being subjected to slavery. Time and again they have turned back to their God, and He has rescued them, returning them to their promised land. The last time was when Israel was reestablished as a nation on May 14th, 1948 and repopulated after their devastation by Hitler. The restoration has been long, painstaking, and bloody, but it has been evident that God has been their champion in such events as the Six Day War in 1967.

Now, after all that time, all the bloodshed, all the taking of territory inch by inch and foot by foot, they are ceding that territory so hard won. Their fight never ceases, they have never known peace. Imagine a child who has never known a day of true peace, a youth, a 40-year-old, a grandmother who has never known a carefree existence, who may have lived in several lands and never known a true home. One cannot help but wonder if it is because they have never opened their eyes and received the Savior, the Messiah that God has sent.

So many Jews refuse to search the Scriptures and compare the Old Testament with the New, to study Christian apologetics to discern whether Jesus is truly the Christ, the Messiah whom they have so long awaited. For if they would do this, they would find that the Scriptures point His way, that He has truly come. Yet many Jews will study the Kabbalah, seeking hidden wisdom that God has not chosen to disclose, and in this way pursue mysticism and even the occult. But they will not, with the same zeal, seriously pursue, study, and investigate the claims and facts about Yeshua, the Messiah. They are set against accepting Him.

There is a cry going out from Israel to bring the Jews home once again, and persecution is mounting in the north, particularly in Russia. It is not expensive to those in modern western society to send a Jew home to the motherland ($300), yet one has to hesitate when one weighs the ceding of territory in Israel back to Jewish enemies. Is God the author of this loss of territory? Is this loss of territory happening because Israel won't receive Jesus Christ, their Messiah? We cannot know. We can only pray. Until then, modern Jewish youth are either lost in traditional religious practices that cannot save them or are embracing the humanistic and pagan practices that the rest of the world is. Only a small minority are Messianic, having found and embraced Christ. How can they find God when God is not delivering them from all of this war and pain? Have they ceased looking for Him, calling on His Name? I think about this sometimes and wonder. Upon what do they base their hope? If they are directed by God to keep the daily sacrifices of atonement and cannot fulfill this on the Temple Mount, the only site God has specifically chosen and designated as the only legitimate place for sacrifices, how do they think that they are making themselves clean before Him? Such hopelessness.

Today it is okay to practice paganism, but less and less acceptable to practice Christianity. Silence falls when one declares, "I am a Christian" in a non-Christian arena, and the whole atmosphere changes. When I try to ask my dear friend about the condition of her soul, a wall goes up. The enemy makes even those who profess to be believers believe there is no heaven—for to believe that means to believe there is no hell—and no hell means no consequences for one's sin, and therefore no need of Jesus.

It is more and more acceptable to be openly gay or to be a single parent by choice, and the nuclear family crumbles and the traditional stay-at-home Mom is somehow seen as inadequate unless she is working herself to death at being perfect. It is considered fine to seek alternative medical treatment (I do not mean to belittle alternative medicine, for I seek such treatments prayerfully myself) but to ask for prayer and believe in God is thought to be weak-minded and "needing a crutch." The New Age is about self-fulfillment. Even something as seemingly innocent as angels have become a cult (Colossians 2:18 specifically warns us of "angelology"); Colossians 2:8 warns us not to be turned aside by the philosophies and deceptions of this sort of secular humanism ("See to it that no one takes you captive through philosophy and empty deception…"). We think these things are new, but they stretch as far back as man's very existence on the planet. For as long as we have existed, so has the deceiver Satan, and he has made his lying presence felt in so many ways.

To find self-fulfillment by seeking and finding yourself in God is considered strange these days. I would be tolerated standing on the corner preaching hatred, but may well be ridiculed or run off the same corner if I wanted to teach the love of God. I could teach witchcraft long before I could teach Christianity. I would be tolerated teaching Christ, but not likely much heeded.

Yet we weep and ask why God allows disasters to strike. I instead ask why He puts up with us as long as He does? We have abandoned His Word, blatantly scorned His ways, lived however we've seen fit and spit in His face. He has the entire force of the universe at His command. His patience is beyond anything I can fathom! I can only say that I don't understand it. Why doesn't He wipe us from the face of the planet? It is only His magnificent love and infinite mercy that sustains us.

> *"The days are coming when I will punish all those who are circumcised only in flesh…and all who live in distant places. For all these nations are really uncircumcised, and even the whole house of Israel is uncircumcised in heart"*
> *(Jeremiah 9:25-26,* NIV*)*.

In other words, God says everyone the world over is putting on an act, pretending everything is great with them spiritually, as though everything is fine between mankind and God, when, in fact, everything is instead very bad. Spiritually, we are nearly destitute the world over, yet we think we are fine—"enlightened." Even many Christians are only going through the motions and scarcely have a relationship with God at all.

During all of this we have never seemed to get it into our heads that the rules governing idolatry and witchcraft are no different today than they were when God banned Satan from heaven before man was created. Satan challenged God's authority and tried to claim a share of His glory and so was banished, for God will not share His glory with anyone except His Son, Who is equal with Him (Isaiah 14:12-15).

> *"When they say to you, 'Consult the mediums and the spiritists who whisper and mutter,' should not a people consult their God?"*
> *(Isaiah 8:19)*.

Consider the shape of the creatures that these false religions represent—the obese and placid Buddha—what is that? Or the Shivas with snaking arms and enigmatic expressions and blank eyes. Are these your gods? Do you have posters, pictures, tapestries, statues of such things in your home? The Israelites and surrounding nations of ancient days did and they were referred to as "household gods." God demanded of them where their gods were when they finally, in their desperation, came to Him for help. Are these the gods you choose to adore? By bringing these representations into your home and setting them up, you are placing household gods just as those people did. There's no other explanation for it. Do you have jewelry or tattoos of these things? You are advertising your allegiance to these same gods. You must clean house.

By accepting the teachings, by repeating mantras that contain words you don't understand you may be reciting prayers to unknown gods. Are you embracing idols and worshipping other gods? You must stop and cleanse your life and home of these influences. These false gods were the reason down through history that God rejected His people. Do you wonder why God sends judgment on His people today when all around us pagan cultures have taken hold and flourish once again? Down through the history in the Bible you can read how each king who followed and pleased God prospered, how each king who followed false gods was defeated. Why are we so slow to learn? Is it stubbornness? Yes, partially. The rest is ignorance of what God's Word says. So let us be clear about what it says.

The first commandment is very specific: "I am the LORD your GOD... You will have no other gods beside Me...you shall not make for yourself an idol in the form of anything in heaven above or on the earth beneath or in the waters below. You shall not bow down to them or worship them; for I, the LORD your GOD am a jealous God…" (Exodus 20:3-5).

We scream and raise our hands, clapping and shouting at concerts and ballgames, but cannot bring ourselves to raise our hands in worship. We allow our teens to plaster their bedroom walls with posters of "teen idols," plainly acknowledging them as such. Don't we hear what we're saying, understand what we're doing, know what we're condoning and closing our eyes to? We are very close to the edge of what God says is wrong, if not over the edge. Have we made gods of these ordinary people? Have we accepted the gods of the world, have we embraced the gods of eastern religions? Have we allowed our children to embrace gods and goddesses of eastern religions and blindly follow witchcraft as a hobby, wandering off into Internet, video and TV land, entertaining themselves with images of hell? Do they read Harry Potter with your permission because you feel they are capable of "separating fact from fiction," and that such "fairy tales" are harmless, when in fact you are condoning what has become a user-friendly Satan?

Cleanse your homes, your hearts, your spirits and your souls, repent and turn back to God because He has turned away from us, His people—because we have turned away from Him first

> "…but your iniquities have made a separation between you and your God, and your sins have hidden [His] face from you so that He does not hear"
>
> (Isaiah 59:2).

We are not playing a game, although our days are awash in games that pull us into the very real world of satanism and spirits. The Internet, video games, board games, TV shows, books and all sorts of pastimes for children are loaded with doctrines of New Age and witchcraft. Yoga, martial arts and Tai Chi, disciplines that are marvelous for the physical body are loaded with underpinnings of eastern religions that are taught along with the physical disciplines; it takes great diligence to make sure the two are separated. If you or your family wish to take any of these classes, you must be constantly aware of what foreign, pagan religious doctrines are being taught in tandem with the physical aspects, and be on your spiritual guard at all times. Such things as massage therapy, biofeedback, acupuncture, and hypnotism for alternative health care are also interwoven with eastern philosophies and if you choose these, you must be diligent at all times to be sure that you are attuned to the Spirit of God and His will. Do not choose these things lightly, but prayerfully and carefully, preferably with a prayer partner aware of what you are doing who will back you up as you enter these risky areas. Optimally you should enter such alternative disciplines with a Christian therapist, if one can be found.

One God only is all we are allowed. If we want to follow the doctrines and teachings of other gods and embrace the isms and principles of gods and goddesses of myth and mythology, we are free to do so—that is a function of the free will that God gave mankind. For, you see, these are labeled "mythology" and are hiding out under the guise of such and are instead, in truth, demons and the work of the enemy of God and our rightful enemy, Satan. We are attracted to these unawares by Satan, for he himself is very beautiful, very attractive, God's most beautiful creation. He comes attempting to seduce us, masquerading as an angel of light (II Corinthians 11:14). We must not be seduced; we must ever be on guard, ever vigilant, ever aware.

We are free to practice witchcraft, to read the future in

the stars, to consult seers and mediums, to call up the dead, to have our star charts drawn. But we do it to the exclusion of God Almighty. If we choose these activities, we choose against God. We will find wisdom there, just as King Saul was able to call up a dead spirit through a witch, a medium (I Samuel 28). Do not be deceived; the power is real power, but it is from a counterfeit source and is limited. Just as King Saul was punished by losing his kingdom and his life, so will anyone who calls on the power of the enemy be punished by God. Why pursue the power of the enemy of God—and that a limited power—when we can ask the Source of All, and have unlimited power in Him? Alas, it is the nature of man to find it easier to take $1,000 in counterfeit currency now than to wait and work for the real thing. Perhaps it is because the pursuit of the counterfeit is intriguing and risky—it gives a jolt, a thrill. Or perhaps the pursuit of the legal tender is too taxing and we are too lazy to go the distance. Christianity is not for the faint-hearted.

Thus, "...wait for the Lord, Who is hiding His face from the house of Jacob," (Isaiah 8:17) is a directive we must seriously heed.

If one must wait, it is because God's face is turned, hidden. And why does He hide His face? Is it because we are unbearably wicked and He, in His utmost holiness, cannot bear to look at us? The answer is a resounding "yes!" Though we trust Christ for our salvation, we must still align our works and our lives with what is pleasing to God or reap the natural consequences of a life without His blessings. Thus we must cleanse ourselves, humble ourselves and approach the throne of grace, beg God's forgiveness and wait for Him to turn back to us and rescue us. Throw off all forms of paganism; there is no other way.

The knowledge of world religions is readily available.

There are volumes of information to be had at the touch of a few keystrokes on the Internet. The problem is that it is perceived as "new" when in fact it is very old; the "New Age" is based on religions as old as mankind. The New Age is based on man's desire to live what he wants to live, to fulfill the lust of his flesh. The first teachings of the antithesis, the direct opposite of the Bible, the satanic bible (upon which non-Christian teachings are all in some way based whether they will admit or not) is that to live to gratify the flesh is the only "good" goal. Personal fulfillment is the only focus and end; lust is to be embraced; greed is justified as natural; even hatred is natural and healthy.

Although most cults seem altruistic, humane, unselfish as you begin to learn them, as you go on you will find that these false religions are based on an egocentricity that states, "I can earn my way into the kingdom. I don't really need God; I can get around my need for Him; I can find my own way in." Jesus Himself said that anyone who tries to gain heaven by any means other than Himself is a thief and a robber (John 10:1).

These so-called religions are in direct opposition to one of the central themes of the Bible: "There is no one who does good, not even one" (Psalm 53:3, NIV).

None of us is fit for heaven and so God has remedied this by making a way for us through grace. Undeserving, we come to Him and He presents us with the gift of salvation through mercy, by giving us the gift of Christ.

Do not be deceived. If you choose the things of false religions, you choose them to the exclusion of the LORD God Most High, for He is jealous God—He even says it of Himself in the first commandment. Read it, recite it, remember it.

"...I, the LORD *your GOD am a jealous God..."*
                                        (Exodus 20:5).

He does not share His people with other gods or powers. He expects complete allegiance. If a secular government
on earth expects complete allegiance of its people, how
much more does the Governor of the Universe expect it of
His people? Only the kingdom of the Most High God will
endure forever, for God has made a way:

"For unto us a child is born, to us a Son is given and
the government shall be upon His shoulders and His name
shall be called Wonderful, Counselor, Mighty God, Everlasting Father, Prince of Peace. ...and of the increase of His
government and peace there will be no end. He will reign
on David's throne (Israel's throne)...from that time on and
forever" (Isaiah 9:6-7, NIV).

So when the flood waters rise, the tsunamis slam into us,
the mudslides wash away the coastline, when the droughts
devour our crops, when hurricanes devastate cities, when
wars will not cease, when epidemics wipe out livestock and
lives, when the red tide plagues the coastlines, when endangered species lists grows day by day, when the ozone layer
dissolves, and we seem on a collision course with eternity,
instead of saying "Why, God?" we must instead say, "Help
us God, we repent!"

Although we should not be unduly afraid of Satan, we
should be aware of what Satan can do in our lives and be
very afraid of what a relationship with him and an alliance
with him now can mean for us in eternity. We should most
certainly not be terrified of our loving and most benevolent
God, but if we persist in following the ways of His enemy
Satan, we make ourselves enemies of God as well, and accept
the same punishment to be meted out to Satan at the end
of time. That is, we will share eternal damnation and hell

with Satan. Do not be deceived, and most certainly do not be naïve. God is not going to overlook your dabbling in the occult, your seemingly innocent idolatry, your playing at witchcraft. You will answer when you stand before Him. If you persist, you will be punished no matter how seemingly holy the rest of your life may be. He will not tolerate these areas of your life and you will be punished. Count on it.

God judged the people in the Old Testament days for idolatry and witchcraft, why not now? He does not change, His Word, His laws, His commandments do not change.

"For all of us have become like one who is unclean, and all our righteous deeds are like a filthy garment; and all of us wither like a leaf, and our iniquities [sins], like the wind, take us away"
(Isaiah 64:6).

"I am the Lord, *that is My name; I will not give My glory to another, nor My praise to graven images"*
(Isaiah 42:8).

"...Before Me there was no God formed, and there will be none after Me"
(Isaiah 43:10).

Look around and consider the blasphemy, witchcraft, murders, sexual immoralities of every kind, idolatries run rampant, greed, lust, corruption, and ask, "Make me clean, Lord!" For it is only with a clean heart, with holiness that we may approach the throne of God and make intercession for our nation and our world. And without such intercession we will surely perish.

Do not compromise. Cleanse your home and do not participate in any form of idolatry, paganism, or witchcraft in any form. Rid your life of these things and repent. Lead your children and friends and loved ones in the same. Take an unbending, unswerving stand. Bring America back to God, to Jesus Christ and to the Holy Spirit. Bring holiness and godliness back to America. There is time yet for us to repent, and repent we must.

Appendix IV:
Basic Holiness

As we walk more and more in faith, we become more confident in our walk with God. When we have a heart that is readily and continually repentant, we can know what God wants us to do with our lives. When our hearts are tender before the Lord we will do well even in the absence of specific knowledge of certain laws and commandments. If we add to that diligent study of the Word and to that, praise and worship and to that, earnestly seeking the Lord in prayer, we will do very well. Because we are more godlike by emulating and imitating Christ as we daily walk in faith, we instinctively desire to live a life pure and pleasing to God, to make our lives as blameless as possible. This is one of the reasons Christ came to earth and lived as a man—to be an example of the way we should and could live our lives in holiness, as God Himself is holy.

As we grow more and more like Christ, we become more and more bothered by seemingly smaller things, things that others may consider insignificant, even considering them not to be sin at all. We continue in this manner as we grow in Christ until we find that we are growing, quite to our own surprise, in some measure holy. Purity of thought begins to overcome the thoughts and troubles of the world and suddenly we find a mind that dwells more on the things of God and less and less on the things of earth. ("To the pure, all things are pure" (Titus 1:15).)

For myself, after almost 30 years with God, I feel God's presence more and more around me, in me, flowing through me. He is there when I wake in the night (Psalm 16:7) and when I get up in the morning, when I'm driving my car, or walking down the road. He's there when I'm singing His praises or laughing with friends and loved ones. There are so many places to find God and so few places to go where He cannot be found, for He is indeed everywhere you go if you choose to make Him a part of your life, for then you will carry Him always within.

I "grew up in church" as one says—where I was brought up by good parents who tried their best to school us in the precepts of the faith and to teach us to know God, mostly by hearing our lessons, for that is what they knew to do. I attended nine years of Catholic school. Most of those years I attended Mass daily. When I attended public school, I attended weekly catechism classes. But for years I blamed the Catholic Church for my sinful ways, saying that they caused my bitterness and guilt, but it was not so. I used the church as a scapegoat, when instead it was simply a case of conscience. There was some fault, however, in that it was supposed that I knew and embraced God naturally, when, in fact, I did not. Care was not taken by my teachers to examine me other than to hear my memorized lessons, assuming that embedding these "catechisms" would do the job. This, I feel, is the vast and most marked difference between the protestant and Catholic faiths. The evangelical protestants like to make sure (for the most part) that their converts fully understand what a true relationship with God entails, leaving nothing to chance, while, it seems, the Catholic church would rather trust that such a relationship will be learned by osmosis. I am not saying that the Catholic church is apostate, in error, but am warning that like any other church, if one trusts in the church and its works rather than in Christ for one's salvation, this is the wrong course.

In addition, I was trained in witchcraft as a young woman by women professing to be Catholic believers. (See the *Appendix III: Paganism in Our Homes.*) Such involvement by their parishioners should be a sign to priests and pastors that there is something urgently amiss within their congregations that must be addressed. The advent of small groups in the churches makes it much easier for pastors to gauge the spiritual temperatures and to keep a finger on the pulses of their flocks. And, we have all heard of corrupt and dishonest pastors taking advantage of their flocks—supposedly devout men and women in the church living openly in sin. This is because these people ministering are like we are, human and burdened with sin, but they are not being kept accountable by partnering with other co-leaders. (Please see the chapter *Faith to Be Led* for an excellent model of Christian leadership.) All of this was a lot to bear for a young person trying to find her way spiritually and I was easily led down the wrong path, and as willingly followed, feeling safe with these "white," or "good" witches, because, after all, they were Catholics like I was. What could be the harm? I justified it thus.

When seeking holiness, such a path does not show well as the one to take, and so I abandoned it as false. Please understand that I do not indict, condemn, castigate and/or denounce the Catholic church or any church body as a whole. I only write this to illustrate that when one puts one's faith in a church and it's doctrine as a method of salvation, that faith is seriously misplaced. There are many church bodies that embrace and/or tolerate sinful beliefs that do not line up with the Word of God that should also be warned. Abortion, corruption in business, casual occult practices (See *Appendix III: Paganism in Our Homes*), sexual immorality, and other modern hot-button issues of the day are nothing but sin still. God's description of sin has not changed because the calendars have taken us through new centuries. God does not change and is still holy.

When we meet God and have our faith well-placed and begin to grow in Him, things very soon happen in our lives. We change little by little; the things we want also change. Our characters undergo change, and bit by bit the things of the world seem less pleasing to us and the things of God more attractive. We think that perhaps we are a bit more godlike—yet we are not pure and holy if we see holiness as God strictly views it, for we can never measure up to such perfection. But we must not let that discourage us, we must ever press on. And even as we do so, we must not think of ourselves as holy, for if we do so, this finds us walking in the sin of pride. Oh weak, sinful creatures, we! It is hard to keep perspective, for in our flesh we are bound to these sinful, unholy bodies, and yet because we are heaven-bound, because we press on toward our reward, we strive toward holiness. So in faith, we try always to please God, to be a bit more holy every day. We can do this by maintaining our proximity to God. By staying close to Him, by keeping His Word in our hearts, in our spirits, on our lips, we grow closer to Him. It is, as in any relationship, inevitable. ("I have hidden Your Word in my heart that I might not sin against You" (Psalm 119:11).) And then finally, we find that we feel we have in some measure become pleasing to God, not because we are perfect and holy, but because of all this striving, because we are constantly trying, because we are what God said King David was, "a man [or woman] after God's heart" (I Kings 11:4).

But there is none righteous, says God in His Word (Psalm 53:1, Romans 3:9), not one. We have all sinned, we all continue to sin. We were born in sin, we are steeped in sin, we continue to sin, for we are human and are surrounded by sin, are tethered to a sin-sick, willful, human nature. No, we are not holy. The best we can do is to treasure, protect, nurture and invest the faith God has planted and wrought, fashioned, formed and created within us for the work of the kingdom. Therefore, we must make every effort to avoid things that will compromise or damage our faith, that will dampen it or lull it into false sense of well-being or rest—anesthetize us to the evil around us.

So we put on the whole armor of God: "...having girded our loins with truth, having put on the breastplate of righteousness, having our feet shod with the preparation of the gospel of peace and with the shield of faith..." as in Ephesians 6:13-16. Then having done all, we stand firm. We do our best to live holy lives.

God's gifts are for all who have faith, for all who believe (Romans 3:22). If we lack faith because we do not take care of that basic gift of faith that led us to first believe, we can not only lose sight of what God can do for us and through us for the kingdom, but we could also lose our very salvation. Indeed "faith without works is dead" (James 2:14), meaning there is nowhere in God's plan that guarantees that a one-time commitment with no follow-through equals salvation. Salvation is by faith, yet each is warned to "work out your salvation in fear and trembling." This means that if we are truly "saved" something has happened in our spirits, hearts and souls. Just as a body that is healed from disease is different, so is a soul that is healed from spiritual death by salvation different as well.

It is certainly true that salvation is by faith, but someone who shows no change, no proof of having ever met or wishing to follow God, may not really be saved. God only knows the true condition of that soul. It is also true that those who meet Christ and zealously follow Him with their whole hearts store up much treasure in heaven. These treasures are fondly referred to as "crowns" and are treasured by the saints as rewards to be brought before Jesus, to be cast at Jesus' feet as gifts for our King when we finally meet Him in eternity.

Christ warns that many will come seeking Him, claiming to know Him, only to be turned aside and rejected by Him (Matthew 7:21-23). Thus must we be careful to continue to work through our faith, to be what we proclaim to be, to "walk the talk." We don't say, "I am saved," then discard what Jesus has done, blatantly disregard His salvation and return, like a dog to his vomit, to our old habitual life of sinfulness in all its vileness. Instead we do what is meant by "working out" the salvation: to prove to others by one's deeds that something has actually happened because of Christ—that one's life has actually changed.

Thus do we rejoice in our suffering. We persevere. Our characters undergo change year by year as God bends us, breaks us, remakes us ("We are the clay, You are the potter; we are the work of Your hand…" (Isaiah 64:8)). Isaiah uses the illustration of the potter remaking an article repeatedly until it comes out right to demonstrate how we are remade again and again—if we are willing. God is gentle; He will not force us. Christ is the Rock of our Salvation; to come to Him wholeheartedly means to fall upon Him full-force, to fall down humbly before Him, to be completely broken by Him and mended and made new, into someone brand new. But He will never break anyone who does not come to Him freely seeking to be refined, refitted to be made more useful. We learn though trial and error, over and over. If we go through a lesson and fail to grasp the whole truth or don't apply what we've learned, we will find ourselves undergoing similar circumstances until we get it right (Romans 5:2-3).

So let us strive to be holy. It is a lofty goal, to be sure, especially since we are already told that there are "none holy." But it is the striving that counts. It's the effort that counts. If we can't be holy, at least we can be that man or woman after God's own heart—a very good and blessed way to live out a faith-filled life.

How to Become a Christian

Becoming a Christian is a very simple matter. All you need to do is acknowledge that you are unable to keep the commandments of God and live a holy life and that because of that, you need help from God. To break even one commandment (for example, to steal one cent, to tell one "little" lie) is to be guilty. Once you have acknowledged that, a simple prayer of confession and acceptance like the following will commit you to Jesus, remembering that "something" (evidence of a changed life) must follow:

"Jesus, I confess that I am a sinner, and I know I can't make it into heaven on my own. I'm sorry for the life I've lived. Please forgive my sins. I ask You to take over. I know You paid the price for me already with Your death on the cross. I confess that I am unable to live this life on my own and ask You to guide me by Your Spirit. Help me to live for You, to grow in You, to learn more of You every day of my life from now on. I love You and I want to make You Lord of my life. Amen."

The first thing you should do after saying this prayer is to tell someone that you've committed your life to Christ, for the Word of God says that if you "confess with your mouth Jesus as Lord, and believe in your heart that God raised Him from the dead, you will be saved..." (Romans 10:9). This is your most important first step as a Christian;

you must confess Jesus as your Lord. That means you must openly talk about it and discuss it with people around you. Making Him "Lord" simply means putting Him first and giving Him preference and control.

Your next step is to begin reading your Bible, starting with the gospel of John. This gospel provides important information about Jesus' life and role before His life on earth, as well as history that the other gospels don't relate. It then tells all about His birth, His ministry, passion and death.

Immediately begin praying and worshipping God on a regular basis, and, if you don't already do so, begin going to a good Bible-believing church. If you need to, review the chapter on *Faith to be Led* to help you find a church.

Find someone that can encourage you in the Lord on a daily basis. If you don't have Christian friends already, talk to the pastor of the church you attend, and he will see that you meet people who will build relationships with you immediately. You will be surrounded with people that love Jesus and will love you because you have made a commitment to Him.

If this does not happen at the church you attend, call the local Christian music station and talk to them and find another church. Get some worship music that you can enjoy. There are many music clubs that you can join where you can build your music collection at reasonable prices. Get some books from the local Christian book store or the library that will help you grow.

The more ways you find to be in touch with God, the faster you will grow in your spirit and the stronger you will be in Christ. Reach out to other Christians and pursue God with all your might. He will bless you in ways you never imagined.

My prayer for you is that this book will help build your faith and that you will live every day of your life blessed by God.